O'Donne WOODTUR TECHNIQUES

D0888572

O'Donnell's
WOODTURNING TECHNIQUES

Michael O'Donnell

Fox
Chapel Publishing

1970 Broad Street • East Petersburg, PA 17520
www.FoxChapelPublishing.com

© 2008 by Fox Chapel Publishing Company, Inc.

O'Donnell's Woodturning Techniques is an original work, first published in 2008 by The Guild of Master Craftsmen Publications Ltd. The patterns contained herein are copyrighted by the author. Readers may make three copies of these patterns for personal use. The patterns themselves, however, are not to be duplicated for resale or distribution under any circumstances. Any such copying is a violation of copyright law.

ISBN 978-1-56523-405-5

To learn more about the other great books from Fox Chapel Publishing, or to find a retailer near you, call toll-free 800-457-9112 or visit us at **www.FoxChapelPublishing.com**.

Note to Authors: We are always looking for talented authors to write new books in our area of woodworking, design, and related crafts. Please send a brief letter describing your idea to Acquisition Editor, 1970 Broad Street, East Petersburg, PA 17520.

Printed in China

First Printing: November 2008

Because turning wood and other materials inherently includes the risk of injury and damage, this book cannot guarantee that creating the projects in this book is safe for everyone. For this reason, this book is sold without warranties or guarantees of any kind, expressed or implied, and the publisher and the author disclaim any liability for any injuries, losses, or damages caused in any way by the content of this book or the reader's use of the tools needed to complete the projects presented here. The publisher and the author urge all turners to thoroughly review each project and to understand the use of all tools before beginning any project.

Contents

Introduction

Pick up a sharp-edged tool and press it against a rotating piece of wood to produce wood-shavings and there you have it – woodturning. It's as simple as that. Of course, it gets more complicated when you begin to learn how to control the tool as it moves through the surface of the wood, exposing the beautiful grain and creating a shape that may have been developing in your mind for some time.

Having the vision to see the finished piece in the wood, before the turning has even started, and then, once you start turning, working in two dimensions to create a three-dimensional object, is a magical experience. It's also a fast process: the wood revolves at up to 2,500rpm; the results are almost instantaneous and there is no going back – once a cut has been made, the shavings can't be replaced.

Goblet with captive rings.

Bowls group.

Then there is that proud moment as you take the finished piece from the lathe and you are able to say, 'I made that.' Even the equipment is interesting, combining technical innovation, such as direct drive electronic variable speed control, with traditional, hand-held tools. Woodturning can also be an extremely relaxing process, working with a natural, beautiful, functional and renewable material. In the workshop, your own domain, the pressures of the day can be left outside. It might be a working environment, but it is also an inspirational space.

If you are interested in taking up woodturning, don't rush into it. The financial investment can be considerable and there is nothing worse than buying the wrong equipment at the start. Make contact with other woodturners, either through clubs, demonstrations, woodworking shows, or seminars, or by taking a course, ideally within a class of three to four students. Taking an evening class at your local college is a good place to start and will give you the opportunity to meet other turners who live in your area. Joining a club adds a social element to turning, while taking part in competitions can create challenges that will help you to further develop your skills.

Once your workshop is full of wood-shavings and the house full of turnings for every occasion, then it is time to think of what else to do with your work. Friends and relations will take care of a few items but you will have to be a little more imaginative for the rest. If the money isn't important, then a charity shop would be very pleased to accept them. Selling your work always sounds like a good idea so that your hobby can begin to pay for itself but it can be a distraction from the woodturning. On the other hand, there is the possibility that woodturning could lead to a new career.

Background

I still have the first two pieces I ever turned. The first was a bowl in iroko, 7½in (190mm) diameter, 3¼in (82mm) tall, turned on a 6in (150mm) faceplate with 1in (25mm) long screws. The base is 1in (25mm) thick. At the time I thought it was wonderful and so did my family. Later on I wanted to burn it, but now I find it most interesting to look back on, even though it has spent many years in the garden holding a plant pot. The second piece was a three-legged stool which I used twice a day for seven years to milk the cow. It now has pride of place in the house. Both pieces were made in evening classes at the local high school, before I had a lathe of my own, in the winter of 1973/4.

Once I had my own lathe, woodturning became part of my living. I made mainly domestic items: lamps, bowls, candlesticks, trays and goblets. I sold them from my workshop which is on the road up to Dunnet Head, the most northerly point on the Scottish mainland. One item I was particularly keen to make was a spinning wheel so that we could spin our own wool. I sold the first one before it was finished and the neighbour who bought it, Joan Glass, won first prize for her spinning at the Royal Highland Show in the 1970s. This in turn created a market for my wheels and they became my best product.

Top My first ever turning piece: a bowl in iroko, 7½in (190mm) diameter. Turned in an evening class at my local high school. Held on 6in (150mm) faceplate.

Middle My second turning piece: a three-legged stool in sapele. I used this for milking the cow twice a day for seven years.

Right Lamp in sycamore.

I had never attempted boxes; back then it was a measure of how good a turner you were – does the top go pop as it is removed? That was until I got an order for 500 apple-shaped boxes, in apple wood, for the *New York Times* in the 1980s. Then it became worth learning. By the time I had made 50 boxes I was really in the swing of it. Ray Key made half the order, which certainly took the pressure off me.

After meeting Richard Raffan in 1981, I began turning green (unseasoned) wood and have been doing so ever since. I started off using interesting woods brought up from Inverness (130 miles south), but after a while decided to use only local woods. As our local wood is mainly light-coloured European sycamore (*Acer pseudoplatanus*), it wasn't long before my wife Liz was working with me to decorate the pieces. We still continue to turn and decorate local sycamore. The images on these pages are mainly early pieces that I made before I began working with green wood.

Top Orkney upright spinning wheel in afrormosia. This was my main product in the 1970s.

Left Spinning chair in afrormosia. These became popular for christening and wedding presents.

Below Lidded bowl in afrormosia.

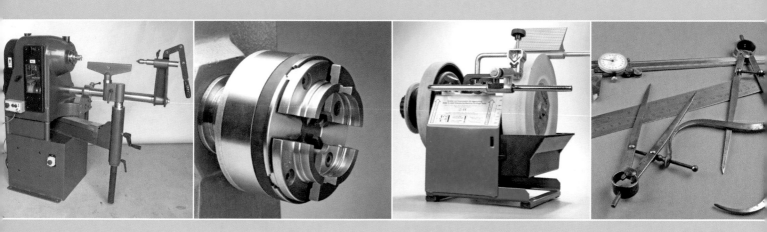

Part one – Equipment

The equipment you buy needs to be appropriate for what you want to make, which could be anything from miniatures to world record sized bowls. In general, most turners want to be able to produce a range of work from 12–18in (30–45cm) diameter bowls or vessels to pens, standard lamps and egg cups. All these are compatible with a carefully selected set of equipment, which we will look at in this section. Once you have the tools and equipment, it is worth taking time to understand them and the turning process. This will not only save you money but, more importantly, will greatly improve your enjoyment and ability in the woodturning shed.

The lathe

The lathe is the centrepiece of the workshop, where the main action takes place and it should be easy, fun and safe to use. When you walk into your workshop, you should have a sense of anticipation about what you will make on your lathe and that you are going to enjoy the experience.

Capacity

The first criteria to consider when selecting a lathe is its capacity. This is the maximum size of wood that the lathe will hold and the power needed to drive the cuts.

A spindle length of 30in (760mm) and a diameter of 4in (100mm) would be adequate for most spindle turning projects. This requires a capacity of 32in (810mm) between centres and a centre height of 3in (70mm) over the saddle or 5in (120mm) over the bed. Turning bowls up to 16in (400mm) diameter over the bed requires a spindle height of 9in (220mm), making an allowance for roughing down.

Outboard turning is very convenient because it allows easy access around the bowl while turning and has greater capacity than over the lathe bed, up to 20in (508mm) diameter. If the outboard threads are the same as the inboard threads then your chucks can be used on both sides. For this to work the lathe must have a reverse switch. For some lathes with

Above The Vicmarc variable speed lathe.

Right The VB36 heavy-duty lathe.

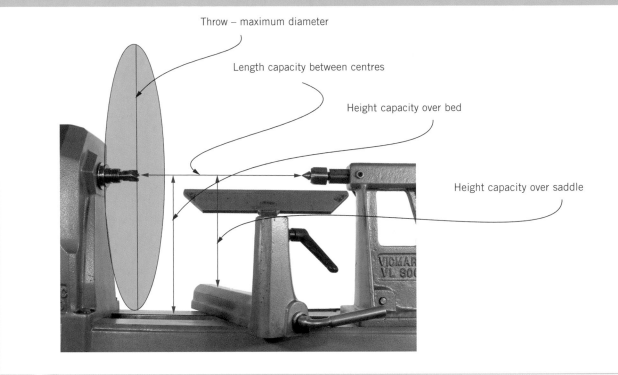

Throw – maximum diameter

Length capacity between centres

Height capacity over bed

Height capacity over saddle

Above Capacity of the Vicmarc VL300 shortbed lathe.

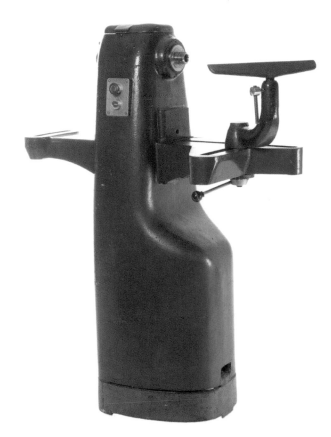

Above The Harrison Graduate shortbed four-speed lathe.

large course spindle threads, such as the Harrison Graduates (1½in x 6tpi), there are dual-threaded chucks that are interchangeable between right-hand inboard threads and left-hand outboard threads.

My first Harrison Graduate lathe was the long bed. I made the decision never to use its outboard turning facility because my right-hand threaded chucks wouldn't fit (and duel threads were not available in the early 1980s). In the long term I decided it would be better to buy a shortbed lathe for large bowl turning, so that my chucks would be interchangeable and, thankfully, this has proved to be the case. My most recent acquisition, a Vicmarc lathe, has a good spindle turning capacity and a greater bowl turning capacity over the bed.

Some lathes have a swivel head, which is a very useful feature. This provides increased bowl turning capacity as you can swing the head up to 90° and work on the same end of the spindle. It is also useful for improving access inside bowls and hollow forms when the lathe is up against a wall or in a tight corner; simply swing the head by a few degrees.

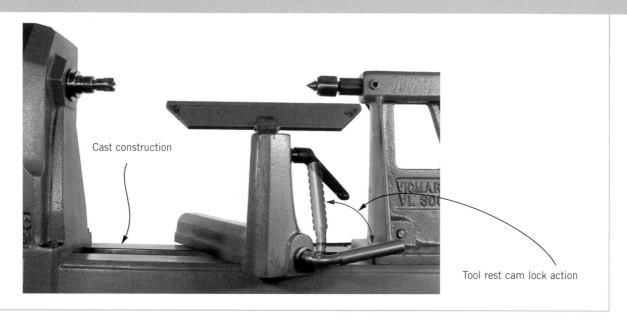

Cast construction

Tool rest cam lock action

Above The cam lock on the saddle is essential for ease of movement of the tool rest.

Power and speed range

The power of the motor has to be a match for the physical capacity. You don't want to be stopping the lathe with a good cut just because there isn't enough power. It's a bit like putting a 50cc engine in a family car when it needs 1,500cc for an acceptable performance.

The motor should be a minimum of ¾hp. More power is usually needed for electronic variable speed drives as they often lack power at the lower speed end (constant torque is not constant power). A combination of pulley change and electronic variable speed is occasionally used to overcome the problem. My Vicmarc has a 1½hp motor, it features variable speed and has three speed ranges.

A good general speed range would be 300–2,000rpm; the high speed is used for small spindles and the slow speed for large irregular bowls. For fixed speed lathes I would suggest an absolute minimum of four fixed speeds, say 300, 800, 1,300 and 2,000rpm. A lathe with more speeds or variable speed would be even better.

I put 2hp motors in my Harrison Graduate lathes, which have four fixed speeds.

Above The Harrison Graduate four-speed lathe.

16

Construction

The weight and rigidity of a lathe are two important qualities we need in a lathe. Together they provide a steady machine, which does not vibrate or move under pressure and is stable when an out-of-balance piece of wood is rotating at turning speed. A cast construction is usually solid; fabricated constructions can be solid too. Don't forget the stand, which should be just as solid as the basic lathe. It should be designed in such a way as to make it possible to stand comfortably close up to the lathe bed or even lean on it while you are working. A large diameter headstock spindle, with large bearings that are well apart, makes for a smooth running lathe.

The switches should be within easy reach from most turning positions; the off switch in particular must be very accessible, especially in an emergency.

If you are planning to turn green wood, which involves the use of water on the wood, then make sure that all electrical parts are well protected from any moisture.

Headstock thread

This should not be less than ⅝in (15mm) in diameter on a small lathe, with registers on the diameter and face for accurate location of chucks and so on. M33 is a good standard thread.

Morse tapers

There should be morse tapers in both the headstock and tailstock so that they will accept standard accessories. A number 1 morse taper is fine for small lathes but they should be a number 2 or 3 on larger lathes, and the same at both ends.

Hollow headstock and tailstock

Hollow the headstock to enable the removal of morse tapered accessories; hollow the tailstock also for removal of morse tapered accessories and for long-hole boring.

Above M33 threads and large registers on the Vicmarc spindle.

Left Work area between centres, toolrest and lathe bed.

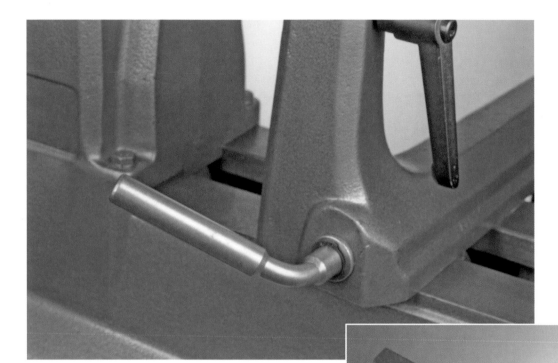

Above Cam-lock on the Vicmarc lathe saddle.

Locking
Cam-locks make the locking action on the tool rest saddle and the tailstock quick, easy and positive. Don't get a lathe without them.

Tool rest
This should have a long, strong straight edge, with a vertical or angled face that will support the tool even when the handle is low. It should taper at the end so that it easily fits into goblets and bowls, with rise and fall 1in (25mm) above and below the centre line.

Above The size, shape and strength of the tool rest is important.

Accessories
The lathe should come with drive and tailstock centres and faceplates as standard.

Some lathes, like the 'One Way', feature a bar along the length of the back of the lathe on which accessories can be attached, such as a local light or a suction point for the dust extractor, even the movable control panel. This can be a very useful feature.

Tip
Only take chucks and tools that are offered as extras to the lathe if you are absolutely sure they are the ones you want.

Chucks and holding devices

There are two basic methods of chucking the wood in the lathe so that wood can be turned. One method is 'between centres', where the wood is held between the headstock and the tailstock with a friction/pressure drive and relies on pressure from the tailstock. The other method is the use of a chuck to hold the wood on one end or face, which does not require the tailstock.

Between centres

Centres are usually fitted into the lathe by means of morse tapers, which can be quickly and easily fitted, then removed with a knock-out bar.

The traditional drive centre has four prongs (or 'dogs') with a fine centre-locating point. This centre point should protrude about ⅛in (3mm) beyond the prongs, to locate the drive centrally, and have a fine point so that it penetrates the wood easily, allowing the wood to be pushed positively onto the prongs. Production turners would use an even longer fine point so that they can mount and remove pieces without stopping the lathe. The drive dogs should have a fine edge so that they penetrate the wood to transmit the drive power. This is ideal for a situation where the end face of the wood is square to the lathe axis, as all four prongs will make equal, positive contact with the wood.

Above Two-prong centre; no. 1 morse taper and 2-1 sleeve.

Right Four-prong drive centre; no. 2 morse taper.

Above Counter bore; no. 1 morse taper with 2-1 sleeve.

Right Steb drive centre; no. 2 morse taper.

Below right Dead tail cup centre used as friction drive; no. 2 morse taper.

When the end of the wood is uneven, or not square to the lathe axis, then the two-prong drive centre should be used; it can be positioned so that both the prongs make equal positive contact with the wood. An alternative to the four-prong centre for smaller work is a 'steb centre', which is a cup centre with a serrated edge. Its advantage is that it only leaves a simple ring mark on the wood, which can be acceptable to leave on for some projects. It is available in various sizes to suit the work being turned.

For special situations there are alternative centres. For instance, when turning a lamp that has a hole bored down the middle, a 'counter bore' would be used. This is usually a four-prong centre with a long pin, instead of a point, which locates in the hole and gives a secure fixing.

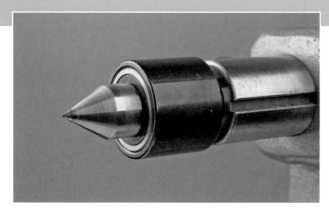

Above Revolving cone centre suitable for hardwoods; no. 2 morse taper.

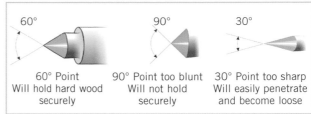

60°	90°	30°
60° Point Will hold hard wood securely	90° Point too blunt Will not hold securely	30° Point too sharp Will easily penetrate and become loose

Above Revolving cup centre with removable point suitable for soft woods; no. 2 morse taper.

Tailstock centres

The tailstock not only supports the wood but also pushes it and holds it firmly onto the drive centre. A revolving centre, rather than a fixed centre, eliminates friction, overheating and burning.

On hardwoods, a simple cone point that penetrates the wood will support it, although the shape of the point is important. A cone angle of around 90° will provide the support and apply the necessary pressure. A fine point (fine cone angle) will penetrate the wood easily; it will continue to penetrate as turning proceeds and the wood becomes loose. A blunt point (large cone angle) won't penetrate enough to hold the wood securely in position under the turning forces and it is likely to come off.

On softwoods, a different design of tail centre is required – a cone point would cause the wood to compress around the cone and to split or become loose. Instead, a cup centre is used; it has a fine point that locates the centre, the ring penetrates to support the wood and the inner cone/flat bottom prevents excessive penetration. The point should be fine and protrude beyond the cup by about ⅛in (3mm) for easy location.

A tail cup centre with a removable pin is ideal for long-hole boring. It can be removed when the roughing down is done, to allow the auger to pass through the tailstock and centre to bore the wood. A straight pin would then be placed in the centre point for a secure fixing.

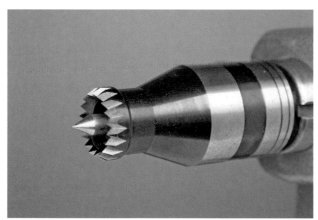

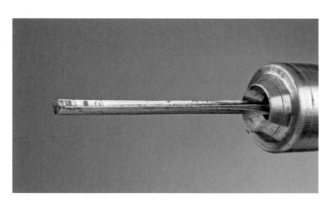

Top left Boring auger through tail centre with point removed.

Middle left Revolving steb tail centre; no. 2 morse taper.

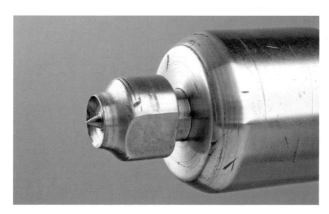

Left Revolving tail centre with changeable drives.

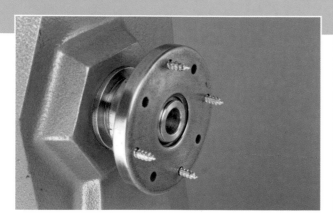

Above 4in-faceplate (multi-screw chuck); four straight holes and four countersunk holes.

Above Forstner bit, used for pin chuck.

Chucks

Hollowed-out items require holding methods that will securely hold the wood on one end or face only, to allow access for hollowing on the other face.

Faceplate

The faceplate (or multi-screw chuck) is the traditional way of holding cross-grain work. It is a flat plate with four or more screw holes, which are either countersunk for standard screws or straight holes for coach bolts. Whichever type of holes are in the plate, I usually drill four more holes of the other type to give flexibility on fittings.

Both 3in (76mm) and 4in (102mm) faceplates will cover most situations, along with a good selection of screws and bolts and a power screwdriver.

Faceplate rings are screwed onto the blank in the same way as a faceplate then held by the expanding jaws of a scroll chuck. This makes them quick and easy to remove from the lathe.

Single screw chucks

The single screw chuck is quick and easy to use and is a good alternative to the faceplate in a number of situations.

The plate should be about 3½in (89mm) diameter, with the centre part recessed about ⅛in (3mm), leaving a rim about ½in (13mm) wide. This ensures that the blank is supported around the rim of the plate for maximum stability, which is important when the face of the wood is not completely flat, or when there is some grain pull-out around the screw.

The single screw chuck has a parallel shank, approximately ¼–⁵⁄₁₆in (6–8mm) in diameter, with a deep, narrow, course thread. It protrudes ¾–1¼in (19–31mm). This is to pull the blank firmly against the plate rim. If the piece to be turned is less than 3in (76mm) diameter, then a plywood spacer can be used to provide suitable support.

The single screw chuck is often the first holding method in a turning sequence for cross-grain bowls. It will also hold on the end grain for small items such as door knobs. A single pilot hole is drilled into the centre of the wood blank, which is simply fastened onto the single screw and the piece is ready for turning. The Sorby off-centre chuck holds the wood with a single screw.

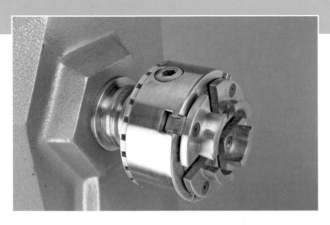

Above Vicmarc VM100 chuck with 2in (50mm) dovetail jaws.

Above Vicmarc VM120 chuck with long nose jaws.

Scroll chucks

The use of a scroll chuck is now the most common method for holding wood. It has a chuck body with jaws that are moved in and out by a spiral gear. The operation is either by key or levers. The key can be operated by a single hand while the other hand locates and holds the wood in the chuck. Once held, both hands can tighten the jaws. The lever-operated chucks require both hands on the levers (unless you are adept at holding one of them against the lathe bed) and your third hand to hold the wood!

Scroll chucks can have a good range of jaw movement, eliminating the need to turn accurate spigots or recesses. There are jaw types and sizes for almost every situation. Most jaws are designed to hold a piece of wood by either expanding or contracting. The contracting jaws grip onto a spigot turned on the blank. The expanding jaws grip in a recess turned in the blank.

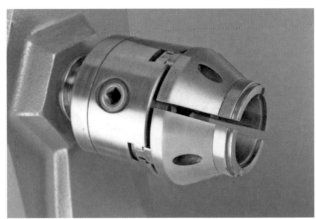

Top Versa chuck with Nova power grip jaws.

Above Axminster chuck with 2in (50mm) O'Donnell jaws.

Left Faceplate rings for use with expanding chuck.

Pin chucks

As the name suggests, this is a large pin, with a secondary locking pin. A bowl blank with an accurately drilled hole is pushed over the pins, rotated in the opposite direction to lathe rotation which locks the blank in position with the secondary pin. To remove, the finished blank is rotated in the same direction as the lathe. This is a secure method of holding the wood and is ideal for natural edge bowls, where there is no flat face for other chucking methods.

A 1½in (38mm) pin, about 2in (50mm) long, is ideal for bowls up to 20in (508mm) diameter (I have turned bowls up to that size on a pin chuck). Even small bowls, down to 3in (76mm) diameter, will fit on the 1½in (38mm) pin. For smaller, dry wood items, such as salt and pepper mills, a 1in (25mm) diameter pin works fine. A 1in pin doesn't work with softwood or wet wood because the very fine secondary pin buries itself in the wood and the blank spins on the main pin.

Jacob's chuck

A Jacob's chuck is most likely to be used in the tailstock to hold drills, but can also be used in the headstock to hold small, round sections, such as dowelling.

Vacuum chucks

Vacuum chucks are a fast, professional production system. They are ideal for holding bowls on the rim so that the bottom can be finished. Or they can be used for flat, double-sided items, like breadboards, without leaving any chucking marks. A vacuum pump is attached to the outboard end of the spindle. A valve releases the vacuum for removing and fitting the piece, which is pushed against a large disk with a sealing surface so it can be turned.

Home-made chucks

One of the pleasures of turning is the challenge of making your own chucks, allowing you to be inventive and save money. If you come up with something good, there could also be commercial prospects. Most forms of home-made chuck are adaptations of existing chucking methods.

Jam chucks

The jam chuck is one of my favourites. I use a small one to hold solid fruit so that I can finish turning the bottom. It is a 20° tapered cup, with a wall thickness of about ¼in (6mm) so that there is some give as the fruit is pushed in. One nice effect is that, as the fruits never go in exactly parallel to the axis, when they are finished they all stand at different angles, which makes them look natural rather than regimented. Don't forget to have a hole down the middle of the chuck so that a piece of dowel can be used to eject the piece. This jam chuck could be held on a faceplate or on a spigot turned on the end.

Above Jacobs chuck; no. 1 morse taper with 2-1 sleeve.

Left Independent 1½in pin chuck on Vicmarc lathe.

Above Blanks for making wooden jaws with Axminster wood jaw plates.

Above Expanding wooden jaws on Axminster chuck.

Wood jaw plates

Wood jaw plates are accessories for scroll chucks. They allow jaws to be personalized for particular applications. I make stepped jaws for holding the rims of bowls while turning the base. Quadrant blocks are screwed to the plates that are then tightened onto a cross. This holds them in their mid-movement position while internal or external dovetailed steps are turned to hold a bowl on the outside or the inside of the rim. The steps are smaller than the jaw's movement so that there is a continuous range from the largest to the smallest. With the cross removed, the jaws can expand into the rim of a bowl and hold it securely.

Waste block

The simplest home-made chuck is a waste block of wood, glued to the bowl blank and used for holding. This avoids leaving screw or chuck marks on the piece, or having to increase the size of the blank to achieve the same result. All you need is a faceplate.

Pin chucks

Even pin chucks can be turned from hardwood, but use part of a nail for the secondary pin. The only limit to the potential of home-made chucks is your imagination.

Above Sorby Patriot chuck with 2in spigot jaws.

Above Jam chuck held in Vicmarc chuck.

Above Tapered mandrill for holding napkins.

Tools

Choosing a set of woodturning tools is one of the biggest decisions to be made, not just because of the cost, which could eventually be more than the lathe, but because they greatly affect the ease, ability and enjoyment of woodturning. A good set of tools will be a pleasure to use and will become the basis for developing skills and making a greater range of products.

When watching professional woodturners demonstrating, it quickly becomes obvious that most of them use very few tools for the majority of their turning. They probably use one tool for most of the time and have a few special tools for their particular style of work. But if you were to take a look in their workshop, the professional might have a great armoury of tools collected over the years, many of them gathering dust; some may never have been used. There will also be some customized tools that do very specific tasks and, while they may only be used a few times a year to remove a very small amount of wood, they are invaluable for that job.

Tip
If you are considering a boxed set of tools, check that they are what you need. There may only be one or two tools in the box that you would actually use. Then again, the price might be right!

Left Form tools for captive ring cutting.

My workshop is no different; there are lots of tools but I use only one, the deep-fluted gouge, for more than 90% of my turning. I also have a number of 'special' tools, which come out for a particular project. A good reason for using fewer tools is that it is easier to learn how to turn. I really learnt to turn when I was making lots of bowls, the majority of which were done with the deep-fluted gouge. I quickly came to understand the tool and then it was easier to understand and use other tools.

Right From left to right: spindle roughing gouge, scraper, deep-fluted gouge, bedan, shallow-fluted gouge, paring tool, oval skew chisel.

A good set of general turning tools should be able to do a wide range of turning: spindle turning ¼–5in (6–127mm) diameter and up to 36in (914mm) long; and bowls from 1½in–20in (38–508mm) diameter. I recommend buying a set of the following tools. See below.

Size	Description	Handle length	Manufacturer's description
1¼in (32mm)	Spindle roughing gouge	18in (45.7mm)	Roughing gouge
½in (13mm)	Shallow-fluted gouge	12in (30.5mm)	Spindle or detail gouge
½in (13mm)	Deep-fluted gouge	18in (45.7mm)	Bowl gouge
1in (25mm)	Skew chisel	12in (30.5mm)	Skew chisel
½–1½in (13–38mm)	Scrapers (various shapes)	18in (45.7mm)	Scrapers
⅛in (3mm)	Parting tool	9in (22.9mm)	Parting tool
⅜in (10mm)	Sizing/beading tool	15in (38.1mm)	Bedan
⁵⁄₁₆in (7.5mm)	Boring auger	6in (15.2mm)	Boring auger

Some of the names I have used for the tools don't match those in the manufacturers' catalogues, because I think tool names should not be unnecessarily restrictive on what the tools are used for and should also take safety into account where appropriate. My 'deep-fluted gouge' is otherwise described as a 'bowl gouge' but I find it absolutely wonderful on spindle work. My 'spindle roughing gouge' is generally known as a 'roughing gouge' but it is one tool that I would not put anywhere near cross-grain work. Not only is it useless for roughing down cross-grain work, I think it is dangerous and I have seen accidents happen. There are some tools, such as the parting tool, where it is appropriate to call them by a 'function' as their use is very limited.

Tool stock shapes and sizing

Round stock – gouges

Sizing dimension

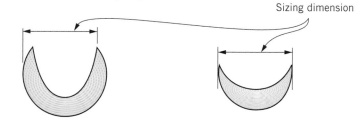

Forged fluted stock – spindle gouges

Spindle roughing gouge

Spindle roughing gouge
(continental style)

Rectangular stock – scrapers, chisels, parting, sizing and beading tools

Scrapers, chisels

Parting, sizing and
beading tools

Oval stock

Chisels

Stock shape

Rectangular or square

Rectangular or square stock is used for scrapers, parting tools, sizing tools and chisels. It's the way the stock is sharpened that defines what type of tool it is. In virtually all cases the bottom corners should be rounded so that they slide easily over the tool rest without damaging it. The 'oval skew' is a further development on rounding the corners and it is a nice tool to hold.

Round

If the stock is round and has a flute then it is a gouge. The shape of the flute determines what type of gouge it is. In general a shallow-fluted gouge is less than a semicircle shape, for taking light and detail cuts, while a deep-fluted gouge has a vee-shaped flute with a small radius in the bottom, greater than a semicircle, for heavier work.

I did have a ¼in (6mm) gouge from round stock where the flute was exactly semi-circle so it was neither shallow-fluted nor deep-fluted. It was a very versatile tool for small detail work as it combined good detail control with effective wood removal.

Forged

Spindle roughing gouges are usually forged with a tang to fit into the handle. Whether the flute is more or less pronounced than a semicircle, it does the same job roughing down spindle work, be it from round, square or from a branch. It quickly removes a lot of wood with relatively shallow cuts and can also leave a very fine finish on large smooth shapes.

The shallow spindle roughing gouge is traditional in Europe; it can also be sharpened with a fingernail grind for detail work.

Size

Chisels and scrapers are sized by the width of the stock. Increased length or thickness over standard dimensions might be referred to as long and strong. Traditionally, gouges were sized by the width of the flute, which worked well when they were forged sections. Now that gouges are generally machined from solid bar, the size definition for the deep-fluted gouge is a hybrid of the diameter and the flute width.

One thing I do say on size is use the biggest tool that will do the job, within reason of course. The premise is that a strong tool won't chatter and can take a large cut; it can also be much easier to refine a turned shape. A ½in (13mm) deep-fluted gouge is unlikely to chatter, even with a 6in (152mm) tool overhang, and if a 1½in (38mm) scraper will fit into an egg cup or goblet it is far easier to refine the shape than using a ¼in (6mm) scraper. The ¼in (6mm) scraper could even chatter with a 2in (51mm) overhang, making a fine cut impossible.

Material

Traditional tools are forged from carbon tool steel and then hardened and tempered to take a very nice cutting edge. However, it doesn't last very long. When sharpening carbon steel, great care is needed not to overheat the tool as it will begin to lose hardness as low as 150°C; at 300°C the structure will be destroyed. This is less of a problem on the newer, cooler cutting ruby and blue ceramic wheels, wetstone grinders and the belt grinders.

Most turning tools are now made from high-speed steel (HSS). Some are forged, but they are mainly machined from square or round stock. M2 is a standard HSS stock; it takes a nice edge and is longer lasting than a carbon steel edge. There is less chance of losing the hardness through overheating while sharpening – as the steel has to reach 580°C, which is most unlikely while sharpening on the correct stone. When grinding HSS never quench it in water or oil; the sudden change in temperature causes thermal shock and results in hairline fractures on the cutting edge. If your tool gets hot, put it down and walk away for a while. HSS in the form of powder metallurgy has a more even distribution of carbon throughout the steel. This can give you a marginal increase in hardness on larger section tools but is rarely used on smaller sections due to the lack of grain structure and therefore tensile strength. Be aware that powder metallurgy steel doesn't guarantee a good tool, rather it is the heat treatment that gives you the hardness and toughness combined. Some manufacturers use a single temper on turning tools, others use a triple temper. Single-tempered powder metallurgy will not out-perform a triple-tempered standard M2. After all, powder material *is* M2. There are a few tungsten-tipped tools, they are long lasting but don't have the same keen edges as carbon or HSS tools and also require special sharpening wheels.

Never make turning tools from old (or new) files, because they are very brittle (hard but not tough). Each cross-hatch mark is a potential fracture point and the small, soft tang is not strong enough to take some of the turning forces.

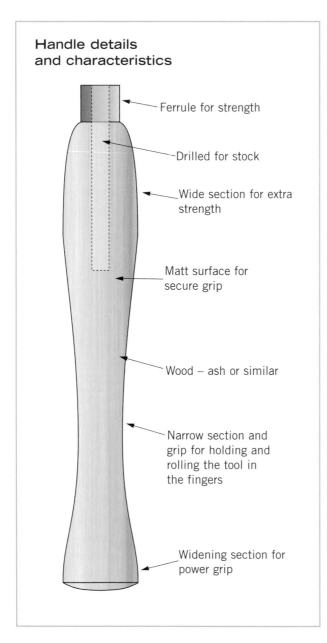

Handle details and characteristics

Ferrule for strength

Drilled for stock

Wide section for extra strength

Matt surface for secure grip

Wood – ash or similar

Narrow section and grip for holding and rolling the tool in the fingers

Widening section for power grip

Handles

Wood is the traditional material for turning tool handles and it is my favourite. Ash is a very nice, strong and shock-resistant wood, but almost any hardwood will do the job. The warmth of wood feels nice in the hand; a natural wood texture provides grip, whereas a highly glossy finish can be slippery. A wide section at the end is suitable for power grips and a narrow section in the middle is a good shape for rolling in the fingers, making detail work and sharpening easier.

The metal ferrule provides strength without bulk. The length of the handle can make the difference between the tool being usable and unusable. Too long and the tool will be difficult to handle, too short and it will need much more force to keep it stable and controllable. I think if most woodturners increased their handle lengths by about 6in (152mm) they would see a great improvement in their turning.

Metal handles are fine for deep hollowing situations where extra length and strength are required.

Angles and cutting edge shapes
Bevel angle

The bevel angle is the angle between the bevel and the axis of the tool. The angle of the bevel has a number of effects. It defines the tool 'edge angle' (except on chisels, which are sharpened on both sides so it is the sum of the bevel angles). It is also the cutting angle on gouges when the bevel is in contact with the wood. The bevel angle determines the strength of the edge – larger angles have stronger edges. A 45° bevel is a good strong edge. Anything less than 30° and the edge is a bit fragile for turning but can be used for a special situation.

The bevel angle also defines the position of the handle relative to the direction of cut. A fine angle brings the handle close in line with the cut, while a large angle brings the handle further away from the line of cut.

When gouges and chisels have long bevels, I would recommend putting on a secondary bevel to improve the tool control.

Effects of bevel angles

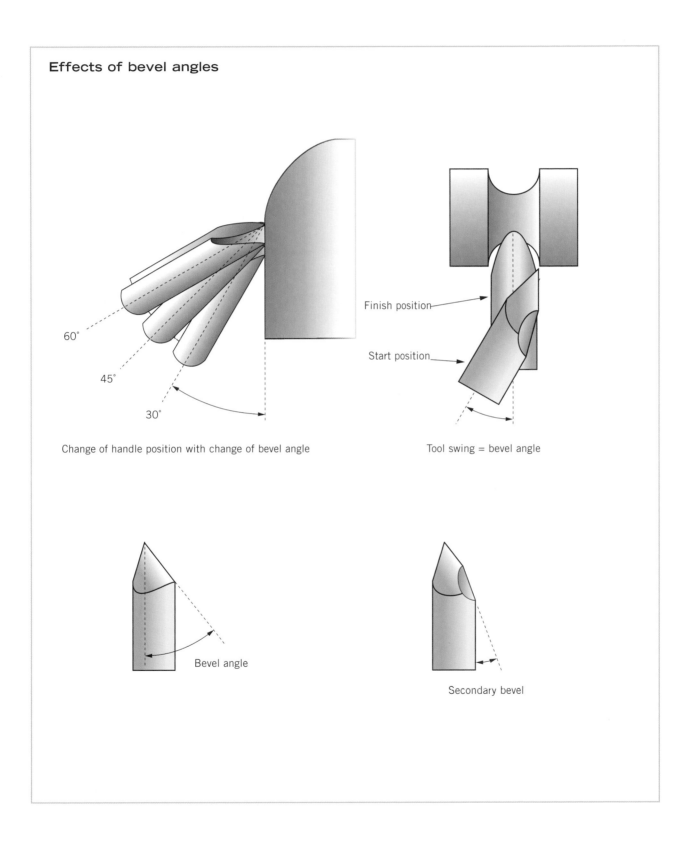

60°

45°

30°

Change of handle position with change of bevel angle

Finish position

Start position

Tool swing = bevel angle

Bevel angle

Secondary bevel

Profile angle

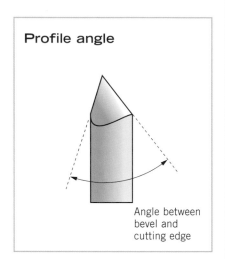

Angle between bevel and cutting edge

Profile angle

The profile angle is the angle between the bevel and the cutting edge. In simple terms it defines the narrowest vee the tool will cut.

Rake angle

Standard scrapers are flat on top, which is a zero rake angle. Adding a negative rake at the cutting edge may reduce the risk of a dig-in.

Effect of profile angle

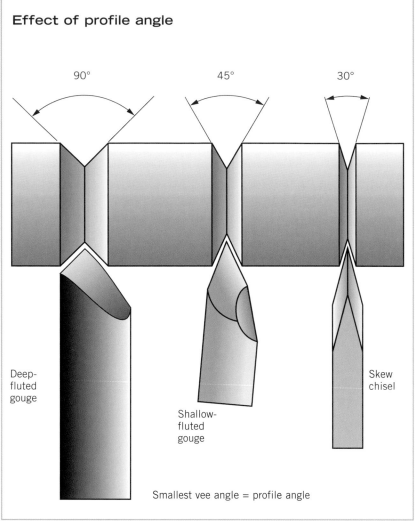

90°   45°   30°

Deep-fluted gouge

Shallow-fluted gouge

Skew chisel

Smallest vee angle = profile angle

Rake angle

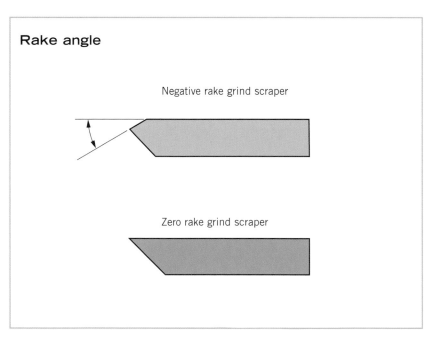

Negative rake grind scraper

Zero rake grind scraper

Skew angle

A skew chisel or skew scraper is one where the cutting edge is not at 90° to the tool axis. The skew angle is measured from the cutting edge to the tool axis. The main effect of having a cutting edge skewed is to change the position of the handle relative to the cutting edge. This can greatly improve tool control and allow access into tight spaces. A good skew angle for a chisel would be 60°.

Effects of skew angle on tool handle position

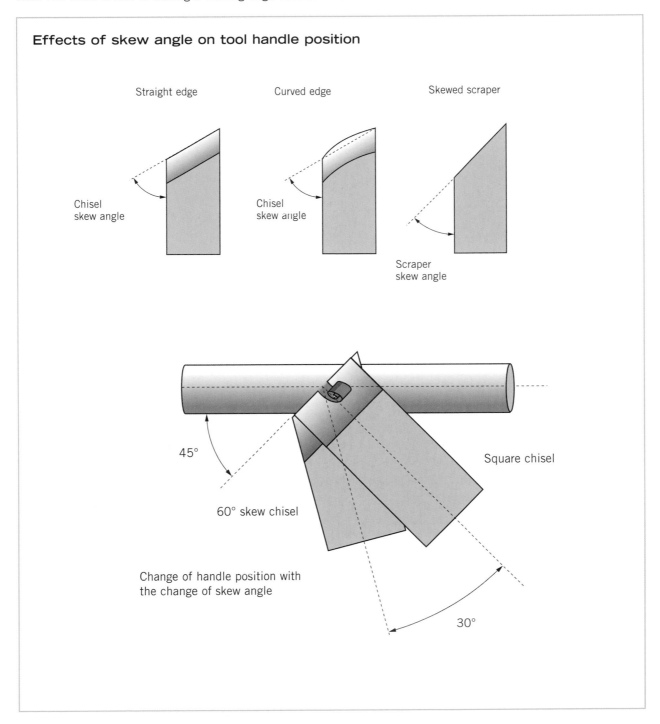

Straight edge

Chisel
skew angle

Curved edge

Chisel
skew angle

Skewed scraper

Scraper
skew angle

45°

60° skew chisel

Square chisel

Change of handle position with
the change of skew angle

30°

Different cutting edge shapes

Fingernail grind on the shallow-
fluted gouge (SFG)

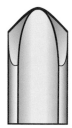

Swept back grind on the deep-
fluted gouge (DFG)

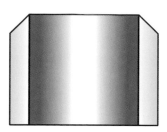

Square grind on spindle roughing
gouge (SRG)

Cutting edge shapes

Cutting edge shapes are very much visual definitions. The **fingernail** was at one time referred to as the 'lady fingernail'. The bevel is not visible from the front of the tool. The fingernail grind is traditional and has been in use for a long time on shallow-fluted gouges. It is a fine detail grind, used for fine detail work.

The **swept back** grind is used on the deep-fluted gouge, where the edge is swept much further down the stock than the square grind. Some of the bevel will be visible from the front, though the shape of the edge will be similar to that of the fingernail grind. This grind was developed in the early 1980s when HSS round stock came into woodturning. It is sometimes known as a 'Celtic' grind.

The **square** grind is where the gouge is just rolled on the platform, creating a square shape as if it had been sharpened with a pencil sharpener. It is typically used on the spindle roughing gouge.

On scrapers and chisels, the cutting edge shape is independent of the bevel and profile angles and any shape of cutting edge can be created on the grinder.

Some scrapers are **form** tools; that is, the shape of the cutting edge is similar or exactly the same as the shape it is cutting. There are bead, cove and vee-cutting tools. These shapes are sharpened on the top of the tool so as not to change the cutting edge shape.

Tool sharpening and care

A turning tool can remove more wood in a few seconds than a hand-plane will remove in a day. A log can be reduced to a pile of wood shavings in a matter of minutes. With wood removal rates like this, keeping the turning tools sharp is a constant job. We should think of tool sharpening as part of overall tool maintenance and care; it is the key to pleasurable and productive woodturning.

Tools not only become blunt with use, but they can also get out of shape; edges can be accidentally damaged. A tool may need reshaping to change its cutting characteristics, even from new. Keeping tools in shape is just as important as sharpening. Shaping and sharpening are similar metal removal processes; pressing the tool against a moving abrasive surface, or rubbing the tools against an abrasive surface creates the same final result – a well-shaped and sharp cutting edge.

An introduction to sharpening systems

With the regularity that turning tools need to be sharpened, a powered sharpening system is called for. There are four basic methods of putting an edge on woodturning tools: wetstone grinders; belt or disc grinders; high-speed grinders and honing. The following considerations, which contribute to the ability of the system to deliver sharp and well-shaped tools, apply to all four systems.

Power There should be enough power for the machine to start quickly and sustain rotation under the heaviest sharpening conditions.

Construction The system should be sturdy enough to take the knocks of the workshop.

Tool rests and jigs A good tool rest and a set of jigs makes sharpening much easier and encourages more regular use. Positive pre-set angles on platforms allow settings to be changed quickly and easily.

Below It is important to sharpen tools regularly.

Surface speed		
Machine	**UK 50Hz**	**USA 60Hz**
8in (203mm) grinder	3,000rpm = 105ft/sec (32m/sec)	3,600rpm = 126ft/sec (38m/sec)
6in (152mm) grinder	3,000rpm = 78ft/sec (24m/sec)	3,600rpm = 93ft/sec (29m/sec)
6in (152mm) grinder	1,500rpm = 39ft/sec (12m/sec)	1,800rpm = 6ft/sec (15m/sec)
Flat belt	2,800rpm (Sorby) = 26ft/sec (8m/sec)	3,360rpm = 32ft/sec (9.6m/sec)
10in (254mm) grinder	150rpm (Tormek) = 6.5ft/sec (2m/sec)	180rpm = 7.7ft/sec (2.4m/sec)

Surface speed This is a major factor in contributing to heat generation, with which we can make direct comparisons between systems. See the table above.

Cutting media Grinders should come with good wheels suitable for high-speed steel and carbon steel tools, or there should be a good selection of media, which can be fitted to allow the turning tools to be shaped and sharpened without overheating.

Cost You can buy a small lathe for the price of some sharpening systems but it should be money well spent if you make the right choice.

Wetstone grinders

Traditionally, the wheels of wetstones were made from sandstone, which has quite a coarse grain (equivalent to about 150 grit), which provided good metal-removing properties. About 2ft (609mm) diameter and 4in (101mm) wide, the wheel would have been pedal-operated and run in a water bath. Wetstones were used for most fine-edged woodworking tools and it would be usual for a joiner to finish the edge of his tools on a flat stone (oil stone).

Modern wetstone grinders are generally 8–10in (203–254mm) diameter and 2in (50mm) wide. They are now electrically powered and run at about 150rpm, with a fine-grit wheel of around 240 grit. Grits as fine as 4,000 are available for some grinders. Water-cooled wheels cut relatively slowly, there is no risk of overheating and the fine grits give a fine

Above Tormek wetstone grinder with jigs and honing wheel.

edge on the tools. In terms of power, I would be happier about some wetstone systems if they were a little more powerful. Wetstones generally come with a reasonably sized adjustable tool rest. The Tormek system has a wide range of jigs for sharpening everything from a pen knife to an axe, with plenty of options for the woodturner.

Wetstone wheels are not generally interchangeable between models and manufacturers, so the wheel that comes with the grinder is often all that is available. The Tormek 10in system has a very sharp 250 grit wheel, which is excellent for straight-edged tools. Curved-edged tools should be continuously moved across the whole width of the wheel while sharpening to avoid grooving. Other systems have harder, but not so sharp, wheels and so keep their shape well but it takes longer to sharpen the tool.

Most wetstone grinders come with a second wheel, which is either in the form of a high speed or a honing wheel. Having a high-speed wheel attached would seem to give the best of both worlds, but in fact it isn't a practical solution as there are a number of serious disadvantages. The main disadvantage is that a grinder needs to be set at a comfortable working height and these are different for high-speed and wetstone grinders. A high-speed grinder needs to be higher than bench level as you work in front of the wheel, whereas a wetstone grinder needs to be below bench level as you work on top of the wheel. To exacerbate the problem, on the combined systems the top of the wet wheel is usually higher than the high-speed wheel. On my set-up there is a 25in (635mm) difference in spindle heights between the high-speed and wet grinders. Also, the diameter of the high-speed wheel can be as small as 5in (127mm), which would give excessive curvature to the bevel. So if you buy one of the duel models, buy it for the wet wheel only and ignore the high-speed wheel.

A honing wheel is a very different proposition as it nicely complements the wet wheel, working at the same height, to give the cutting edge that extra polish.

While wetstones may be considered to have a slow metal removal rate, putting an edge on a tool is a relatively quick process. Having a secondary bevel on the tool – just like the joiner with his chisels and plane irons – reduces the surface area being ground, which speeds up the sharpening process. Large diameter wheels – 10in (254mm) – produce a flatter bevel than smaller wheels.

Dressing a very slow running wet wheel is best done with a wide cutting surface such as a devil stone or a diamond cluster in a holder. Using a single point diamond is like playing a long-playing record.

Cost is always relative to what you get and, while wetstone systems appear to be significantly more expensive than high-speed systems, at least you generally get a complete working system.

Belt and disc grinders

While belt sanders are mainly used by woodworkers for sanding wood, Sorby now make one specifically for sharpening woodturning tools. It is not a new idea as some tool manufacturers use belts for tool shaping and sharpening in their production process and some woodturners have also used them for tool sharpening. Belts and discs have a number of significant advantages: they leave a flat bevel on the tool; the belts keep their shape and don't need dressing, and they can be quickly changed for different applications. The Sorby system has a calibrated tool rest, with guides for accurate and repeatable sharpening, and a bar to take their jig for swept-back and fingernail grinds. There are also other polishing wheels that can be attached. The big development is the range of belts available, from

Below Sorby belt sharpening system with zirconium belt and jig.

aluminium oxide to zirconium, in a selection of grit sizes. Belt sharpening systems may well offer an alternative to both the high-speed and wet systems. They could also be used to sharpen 'form tools' on the top surface so that they keep their shape. However, they are expensive: the cost is closer to the price of a 10in (254mm) Tormek wetstone system than that of a high-speed grinder.

High-speed grinders

High-speed grinders are usually 6–8in (152–254mm) diameter and run at 3,000rpm (3,600rpm in the USA). They are double-ended and two different wheels are available. These high-speed grinders are traditionally engineers' tools, but they have become popular in the woodworker's workshop because they will reshape and sharpen woodturning tools quickly and the basic machine is inexpensive.

It is a good workhorse if the power is at least ½hp (375W) for a 6in (152mm) diameter grinder, so that it quickly gets up to speed and has the power for heavy reshaping work. But the basic machines fall down for the woodturner. One problem is the tool rest, which is meant to provide a stable surface on which the tool will rest while sharpening. Most – dare I even say 'every' – high-speed grinder comes with the flimsiest bit of bent metal as a tool rest. This is most unsuitable for the woodturner and should be the first thing to change. A tool rest of 5 x 2½in (127 x 64mm) is a good size. It also needs to be easily adjustable to cover the range of bevel angles at which the tools are sharpened. A variable angle platform uses either a gauge or eyeball to set the angle, which can be relatively accurate although not repeatable. But it is a great improvement on what is supplied. A tool rest which is calibrated with pre-set angles is very quick to set and gives totally repeatable results. A slot in the platform face provides a guide for tool guides and dressing the wheel.

Adjustment for wheel wear – which can be up to 1in (25mm) on its diameter – is essential to maintain accuracy. To maintain a consistent gap between the platform and the wheel there needs to be space between the wheel guard and the motor for the platform to follow.

Below 6in (152mm) high-speed grinder with 80 and 46 grit ruby wheels and O'Donnell sharpening system.

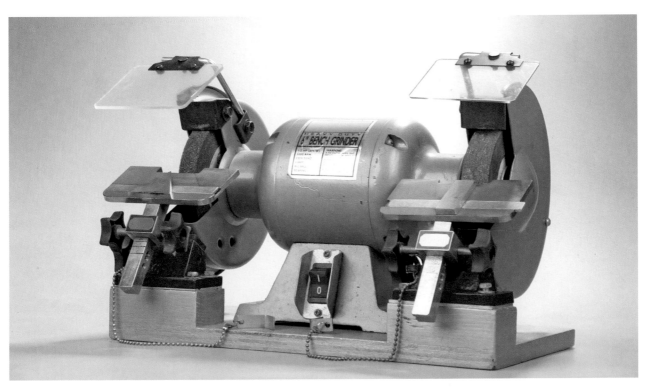

Sharpening some tool grinds on a flat platform, such as a swept-back grind on the deep-fluted gouge, requires quite a bit of practice, so a special jig for that tool is justified for those who are not turning on a daily basis.

Having two wheels is where the high-speed grinder scores highly. There should be one fine wheel, about 80 grit, for putting the edge on a tool, and one coarse wheel, about 36–46 grit, for reshaping tools. If the wheels supplied on the grinder are grey, then they should be changed to something suitable for high-speed and carbon steel tools.

There is generally a much better selection of wheel widths and grits for 6in (152mm) diameter grinders than other diameters. Most grinders have ¾in (19mm) wide wheels, which I consider to be adequate. A 1in (25mm) wide wheel is nice; 1⁹⁄₁₆in (40mm) wide is extravagant and takes more looking after. There are now 1in (25mm) wide wheels recessed to ¾in (19mm) so that they will fit on the shaft exactly the same as a ¾in (19mm) wheel, providing there is space within the guards. An alternative arrangement would have fine wheels on both sides and different jigs in front of them.

In terms of cost, once the rests and wheels have been changed, then the initial advantage of the high-speed grinder being an inexpensive option becomes questionable. Half-speed grinders running around 1,500rpm give a slower and more controlled grind but are generally twice as expensive.

Below Various wheels for the high-speed grinder.

Grinding wheel abrasives

Aluminium oxide is the most common base for grinding wheel grits; the manufacturing process and the additives to the grit determine its cutting and wearing properties.

Grey This very hard-wearing, non-friable grit keeps its shape well. It is suitable for rough grinding of ferrous materials – the wheels are almost indestructible. It is commonly referred to as Carbarundum, which is actually the name of a manufacturer not the material.

White This is a sharper grit than grey. It is 100% friable, originally for surface grinding, easily takes a shape when sharpening gouges.

Pink This is similar to white but sharper and less friable.

Ruby This is a 50% friable grit which is sharper than pink, cuts cooler and keeps its shape better.

Blue Blue has the same properties as white, but with a blue bond.

Ceramic blue This is a ceramic grit that looks like blue aluminium oxide, but is sharper than the best of the aluminium oxide wheels. Each grit breaks into 16 pieces for a constant sharp surface compared with three pieces of the aluminium oxide. It keeps its shape in a similar way to ruby grit. It is a cooler cutting wheel and can be used up to 100 grit on a 3,000rpm grinder.

Silicon carbide green This grit is specially formulated for sharpening tungsten carbide tools, although it will also sharpen high-speed and carbon steel tools. It is very soft and takes a shape easily.

I would suggest ruby grip for shaping and sharpening carbon and HSS woodturning tools – 46 grit as a rough wheel for reshaping and 80 grit for sharpening. You could even go to 100 grit on a slow-speed grinder. Ruby grit is a good working wheel for the woodturner. If you are looking for that extra-fine edge then a blue ceramic wheel with 100 grit will do the job, but white is also good.

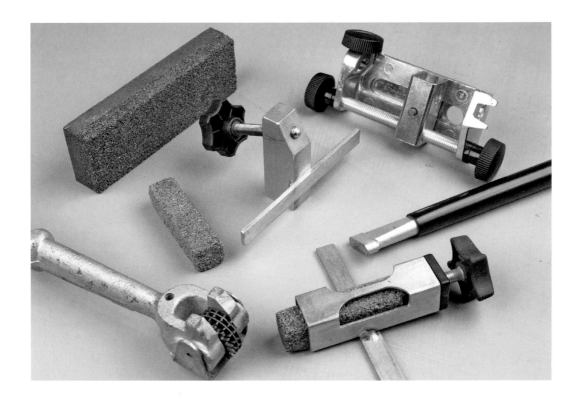

Other characteristics

Grit size Grit size is measured in the same way as for abrasives. The larger the grit, the cooler the cutting.

Hardness This is the ratio of bond material to grit on a volume basis: the more bond, the harder the wheel. Hard wheels wear very slowly.

Openness This refers to the number of air gaps between the grains. Openness is achieved by including a combustible material (it used to be wood-shavings) in the mixture before firing; the more combustible material, the more open the wheel. Open wheels reduce the 'loading' of material on the wheel surface and therefore produce a cooler cut.

Friability This refers to the amount the grain breaks up while in use. Friability of 0% means the grain does not break up at all. At 100% the grain readily breaks up, producing new cutting edges. This is a function of how the grain is manufactured. A friable

Above Clockwise from bottom left· Huntington wheel, Devil stone, O'Donnell single point diamond dresser in holder with guide, hand-held diamond cluster and a devil stone in guide holder.

wheel renews the cutting edges as it is being used. A 50% friable grit is an optimum between the extremes giving a balance between renewing the cutting edge and maintaining the surface shape. While it is useful to know what these properties are, it is unlikely that there will be an option for anything except type and size of grit.

Dressing the surface

The surface of the wheel needs to be dressed on a regular basis to keep it sharp, clean and flat. A blunt and dirty wheel will not do a good job of sharpening your tools and it will generate more heat. Dressing can be done in a number of ways, all of which improve the surface of the wheel but produce different results.

Devil stones

The simplest dressing stick, this hard block of abrasive looks similar in structure to a grinding wheel. Hand-held, it should be slid from side to side across the wheel until the surface is clean. It can also be used in a holder in the guide slot of the platform. The result is a sharp, clean and smooth surface.

Huntington wheels

These are a series of wheels in a holder that is hand-held on the tool rest. The wheels are slid across the surface of the grinding wheel until it is clean. The wheels break up the surface of the grinding wheel to leave a very clean and sharp, but aggressive, surface.

Diamond cluster

Similar to the devil stone but made from industrial diamond, this is hand-held and slid across the tool rest, leaving a smooth and sharp surface.

Single point diamond

These should be in a holder in the tool rest slot. The single diamond cuts the grit, leaving a clean, sharp surface that is parallel to the platform slot.

Honing

Tools such as a 'Form tool' are sharpened on the top face, not the bevel, to keep their shape. A diamond file or flat stone, which has a flat surface, is ideal for this. Flat stones are the traditional method for finishing the edge on woodworking tools that have a very narrow grinding surface, such as chisels and plane irons. Flat stones are available in many different materials from natural stone to ceramic and diamond. Grits range from 400 to 4,000. They could be used to put a fine edge on straight-edged tools like the skew chisel.

Most woodturners use their tools straight off the grinder, but if you want an extra polish to the edge then you might want to hone it.

Left Diamond files and flat stone.

To achieve a mirror-like surface use a felt-polishing mop, loaded with a polishing compound, on a high-speed grinder. Polishing mops are made from felt or fabric, either stitched or unstitched. Use a 'hard' wheel to avoid rounding the bevel at the cutting edge. Alternatively, use a leather strop.

Summary

The requirements of the woodturner are particular in that turning tools are thick, require a robust edge for the heavy work they undertake, and therefore need sharpening quickly and regularly. Wetstones, belts and high-speed grinders will all put an edge on a tool. Woodturners also need to reshape tools to suit their particular application; even changing a bevel angle means removing quite a lot of metal. Both high-speed grinders and belt grinders are capable of removing a lot of material fast. It is this capability that makes them suitable to form the basis of a sharpening system within the workshop.

When the tools are in shape (or close to it) then a wetstone system can add that extra fine edge. In many workshops a complete sharpening system would consist of two different systems. Making that choice is largely down to personal preference. So what do I use? Well, for the past 30 years I have used high-speed grinders, now with ruby wheels and a calibrated tool rest. But recently I have started thinking about adding a wetstone and a belt grinder for some of my tools.

Below Flat stones: ceramic; water stone; oil stone.

Abrasives

Abrasives are sharp grains of various materials that can be used to wear away another material. There is a large selection of materials offering different cutting properties to meet the wide variety of applications used in industry. They also come in a regular range of sizes, which affects removal rates and surface finish.

Below Coated and bonded abrasives.

Aluminium oxide

This is a synthetic mineral (man-made grain), which comes in a number of different forms.

Blue/grey Regular aluminium oxide with 35% titanium oxide. Highly resistant to wear and extremely durable, it is used for high-speed grinding and finishing of metals and other high tensile strength materials without excessive fracturing or shedding. In this respect, grey aluminium oxide will outperform all other bonded abrasive grains.

Brown A lower fired version of blue/grey aluminium oxide.

White This is 99% pure aluminium oxide. It has sharp grit and is 100% friable.

Pink The same as white, with less than 0.3% chromium, which gives it the pink colour and makes it less friable than white.

Ruby The same as white, with more than 0.3% chromium, which gives it the ruby colour and makes it sharper and less friable than pink.

Blue The same as white but using a blue bond.

Ceramic

This is a specially manufactured crystalline abrasive, structured for high stock removal when grinding exotic materials. It is visually similar to blue/grey aluminium oxide.

Garnet

The garnet used in coated abrasives is Almandite, a reddish-brown mineral of medium hardness. It has good cutting edges, which tend to break or re-fracture in use, forming new cutting edges. It is used as a wood abrasive.

Flint

This mineral is quartz (silicon dioxide) and is white in colour. Finely ground, it has the appearance of white sand and fractures into a sharp-edged grain. It is not a good abrasive, even though it is the abrasive used in common sandpaper.

Emery

Emery is a natural mineral composite of iron oxide and corundum. It is black in colour and its grains are hard, round and blocky in structure. It cuts slowly and tends to polish the material being abraded; it is used primarily in the automotive industry. There are natural emery mines in Turkey – the only ones in the world.

Silicon carbide

A very friable grain, silicon carbide cuts faster under light pressure than any other grain used in coated abrasives. Dark green high purity is for sharpening tungsten carbide-tipped tools. Black is used wet or dry for sanding between finish coats, especially on metal surfaces. It has flexible, tear-resistant backing. Silver grey is a very hard, sharp, man-made abrasive suited for non-ferrous materials and non-metallic materials, such as concrete, marble and glass.

Zirconium

Zirconium is a very fine, dense, man-made crystalline grain, which can be used for aggressive stock removal. It has a unique self-sharpening characteristic and so has long life on heavy stock removal operations.

Vegetable

As a complete contrast to the above, vegetable products such as cob husk and walnut shells are used for abrasives, mainly as blast media.

Grit

The crude grains are crushed and separated into sizes, called grit sizes, using calibrated screens. The size is the number of openings per linear inch in a controlled sieving screen, through which the grains fall. Grits range from 12, which is very coarse, through to 1,200, which is very fine.

Below A selection of different abrasive grits.

Auxiliary equipment

While the lathe, tools, chucks and sharpening equipment are all needed for woodturning, there are other items of equipment that are necessary to complete the process.

Measuring equipment

A steel rule for measuring, dividers for marking out and callipers for checking diameters are all useful. Two or three pairs of callipers will come in handy for times when there are a number of sizes to check. For accurate measurement on small spindle work a pair of vernier callipers are useful.

Power tools

A battery-operated screwdriver is essential if you are going to use faceplates. An electric drill can be used for power sanding.

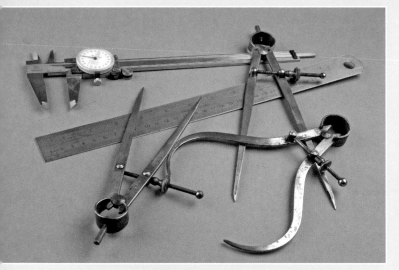

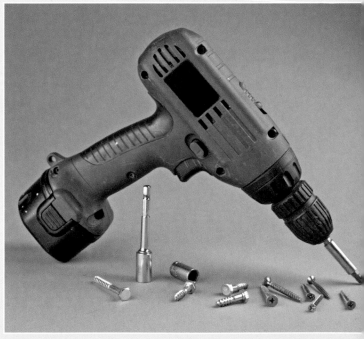

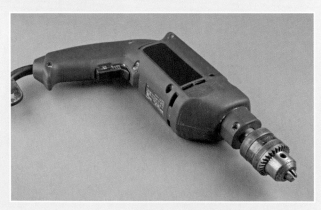

Top left A selection of measuring devices.

Above Power screwdriver with sockets.

Left Bosch mains drill for power sanding.

Saws

In the beginning, no doubt, there is a case for buying all your blanks cut to size ready for mounting in the lathe. But after a while you may find this restricts what you can make and it will also become expensive. So at some point it is worth taking a look at the various types of saws available, to enable you to prepare your own woodturning blanks.

Bandsaw

If bowl turning is your main direction then a bandsaw is essential; use it for cutting circular bowl blanks, ready for mounting on the lathe. It will also be ideal for the preparation of green wood. Check the depth of cut, the throat and the power of the machine.

Circular saw

If spindle turning is your main direction then you will need a circular saw (or chop saw) for preparing straight and square blanks. It is also ideal for making furniture parts, such as legs, particularly when there is a square section left on the leg. Check the machine's blade diameter and depth of cut.

Chainsaw

If you wish to use fresh wood from trees or logs then a chainsaw is the answer. You can even cut down the trees yourself but take some training first and wear the appropriate protective clothing. An electric chainsaw might be all right for small work close to a house but petrol chainsaws are bigger and can be used anywhere.

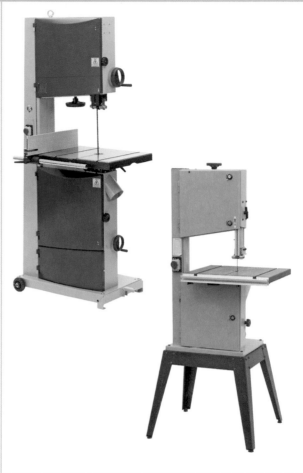

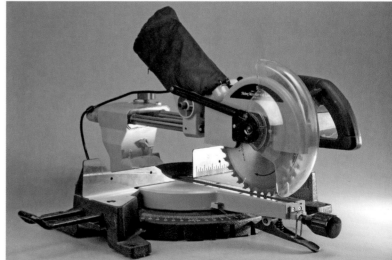

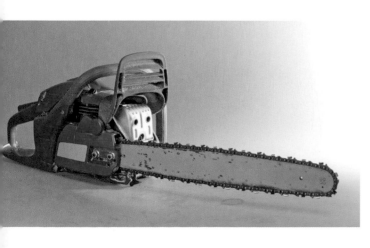

Top Record bandsaw and the Perform bandsaw.

Above SIP circular saw.

Left Hasqvarna 18in petrol chainsaw.

Drills

A pillar drill will be a great asset, particularly when you are making furniture that requires accurately drilled holes. Check the throat depth and drill capacity; a tilting table is desirable. I found a pillar drill invaluable when I was making spinning wheels, spinning chairs and stools.

Air compressor

High pressure air is a very useful commodity in the workshop and can be used for spraying; for powering tools (which is safer than electric, especially when there is water around); cleaning the work while turning; even making a spotless job of cleaning the workshop. A compressor with a reservoir delivers a more even pressure. Small compressors are relatively inexpensive; I couldn't manage without one.

Above Fern pillar drill.

Left Jet air compressor with spray kit.

Below Air blower for cleaning the workshop.

The wood

Colour, texture, pattern, aroma, feel, practicality and availability are all the properties of wood that bring us to turn with it. And, hopefully, sustainability is a property we all look for now. Wood can come from anywhere, from our back gardens to a tropical rainforest on the other side of the world; and can be in many forms, from logs to kiln-dried blanks which are ready for mounting on the lathe. But whatever state the material is in when we buy it, it all comes from trees.

Trees are classified as either hardwoods or softwoods, but names of these categories can be a little misleading as they don't refer to the physical hardness of the wood. Balsa, for example, which is the softest of woods, is in fact botanically classified as a hardwood. Hardwoods have broad leaves, are mainly deciduous and bear a seed, which is contained in a shell or fruit. Softwoods are mainly evergreen, have needle-like leaves and produce an open, unprotected seed usually contained in a cone. There are over 20,000 species of hardwood around the world and over 600 species of softwood. Although there are many temperate countries where there is a

Below 1 rosewood; 2 rosewood; 3 Macassar ebony; 4 ash; 5 bubinga; 6 Honduras rosewood; 7 spalted sycamore; 8 Indian rosewood; 9 Huon pine; 10 apple; 11 yew; 12 cherry; 13 apple; 14 Irish yew; 15 Indian rosewood; 16 Irish yew; 17 birch.

mixture of hardwood and softwood trees, depending on soil conditions, their natural habitats are different. Softwoods are hardy and found in cooler climates with poor soil conditions, while hardwoods are found in temperate to tropical climates.

A tree is made up of a series of rings, from the pith in the centre to the protective outer bark. In temperate climates, growth is seasonal and starts in the spring as the new leaves are formed. The cambium layer (a single cell layer situated between the bark and the sapwood) divides to produce new sapwood on the inside and new bark on the outside; this continues until the end of the growing season in autumn. But there are differences in structure and colour between the wood that is produced in spring, known as 'early wood', and the wood that is produced later in the season, known as 'late wood', which gives rise to the distinctive annual growth rings. The width of each growth ring gives an indication of the growing conditions each year; periods of drought produce little or no growth, while good growing seasons produce a lot of growth and a wider ring. As the tree grows, some of the sapwood no longer required for transportation of sap becomes 'heartwood' and stores waste and sap for lean times. The heartwood of many species also changes to a much darker colour, which contrasts with the usual creamy sapwood.

Above
Numerous burr growth on an elm tree gives a wonderful figure.

Right
Bark markings for crotch figure or possible bark inclusion.

Suitable timbers
Softwoods such as pine, spruce and redwoods are more often used for spindle-turned items – furniture legs, lamps and egg cups. Softwood has one property that hardwoods don't: it is non-porous, which makes it ideal for goblets. It isn't true to say that softwoods are not decorative – yew is a softwood and it is one of the most attractive woods available.

Hardwoods can be used for almost anything – from breadboards in sycamore to bowls and vessels in exotic woods, such as pink ivory.

Most timbers are suitable for turning. Whatever species of timber you choose, it will have different properties from the next. Check what is available in your area and choose something that you like and that is suitable for what you want to turn. If the price is right, then a wood is worth trying – you may discover one that you love. Remember that exotic wood is only a wood from someone else's back garden

in another country. In the UK, for example, African blackwood is an exotic wood, whereas in South Africa sycamore would be considered exotic.

Figure
In a tree with a straight trunk the grain is straight, even and normal for the species. **Figure** is irregular grain from areas of the tree such as the crotch between branches, burr growths on the side of the tree, or high stress areas from tree movement in the wind – such as a short section where the tree emerges from the ground. Some sycamores have unexplained figure, known as **fiddle back**, which is highly prized by musical instrument makers. A **burr** is usually a bulbous growth on the side of a tree, made up of what look like bud eyes, with no particular grain direction. This is a very decorative material.

Popular timbers

African blackwood
Traditionally used for musical instruments such as flutes and whistles. It is close-grained, heavy and black.

Beech
A very close-grained wood used extensively in furniture, it turns well and can be dramatic when spalted.

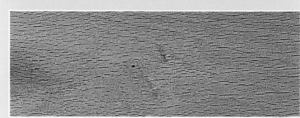

Box
So-named because it was used by the Victorians for boxes. It has a close, fine grain and most of what is available is in branch form, which makes it ideal for box-making.

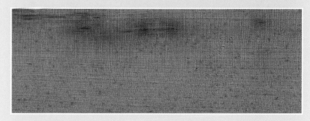

Common ash
A strong, shock-resistant wood with a well-defined grain pattern. It is great for salad or fruit bowls and tool handles. It can be steam-bended and turns well on the lathe.

Fruit wood
Fruit woods such as apple (shown right), pear, plum and citrus have colourful grains and turn very easily. Stable when dry but care should be taken when wet and drying.

Holly
One of the most delightful woods to turn when really fresh.

Laburnum

A small tree that has colourful wood with high contrast between the sap and heartwoods; turns nicely. Avoid the leaves and berries, which are poisonous. A good alternative is hawthorn.

Oak

Mostly used for turned furniture parts and architectural pieces. A good alternative is elm.

Sheoak

A species of Casuarina. It has a fine texture and interesting figure, created from the rays and creamy sapwood that are clearly defined from the darker red/brown/yellow heartwood. I find that it turns very easily.

Sycamore

A white, close-grained wood that turns well. It is the only wood that is guaranteed not to taint food and is therefore very good for domestic items, such as cheese- and breadboards. As a plain wood it lends itself well to surface decoration. I turn 95% of my work from sycamore. Good alternatives are maple and jacaranda.

Yew

A most beautiful wood with a close grain that turns easily. Very decorative for spindle-turned items such as bud vases, candlesticks and spinning wheels. Being a softwood, care has to be taken when sanding as it is liable to heat cracking, particularly on the end grain of bowls and goblets.

Moisture content

When a tree is growing it contains vast amounts of moisture, called sap, which is the lifeblood of the tree. The measure of moisture it contains is its 'moisture content' (MC); this is a ratio of the weight of moisture in the tree to the oven-dry weight of the wood, given as a percentage:

The moisture content can be anything from 30 to 400%, depending on the species. Once the tree is cut down and slabbed it starts to lose moisture to the atmosphere. Moisture loss occurs rapidly at first, then slows down as the moisture content approaches what is known as the 'equilibrium moisture content' (EMC). At this point moisture loss stops, because the moisture in the wood is in equilibrium with the moisture in the atmosphere. Local conditions of temperature and relative humidity determine the level of the EMC, which can be as high as 20% in a damp, cold atmosphere and as low as 2% in a hot, dry atmosphere.

Wood that has been freshly felled is known as green or fresh; it is usually in the round and still full of sap, with an MC of 30–400%. Air-dried wood is slabbed and stacked with spacers, sheltered from the weather (sun and rain), with good natural air flow and allowed to dry. Maximum wood thickness for air

Equation

$$\frac{\text{weight of moisture in the tree}}{\text{oven-dry weight of tree}} \times \frac{100}{1} = \% \text{ MC}$$

or

$$\frac{\text{weight of tree} - \text{oven-dry weight of tree}}{\text{oven-dry weight of tree}} \times \frac{100}{1} = \% \text{ MC}$$

drying is usually 4in (101mm) and takes about one year per inch (25mm). Wood that is thicker than 4in (101mm), or in the round, is more likely to go rotten before it dries.

Kiln-dried wood is slabbed or planked timber put through a kiln-drying programme to bring the MC down to about 8%. It may be partly air-dried first, to reduce costs of the kiln process. Moisture content of 8% is close to the EMC we would expect to find in a house with central heating, making it stable in the home environment. As this is an industrial process, which can take up to four weeks, it considerably increases the price of the wood. It is usually uneconomical to kiln-dry wood over 3in (76mm) thick. If you cut up a kiln-dried plank into blanks then seal the blanks immediately, unless you are going to use them within a few days.

Left A stock of waney-edged cherry boards drying in stick.

Shrinkage and distortion

The removal of moisture from wood causes it to shrink. The main problem with this is that the wood shrinks differently in three directions: longitudinal, radial and circumferential; the last two cause the most distortion.

The longitudinal shrinkage is minimal – on average, around 0.1%. The radial shrinkage is about 2%, on average. If the circumferential shrinkage were also 2%, then the circular section of the log would uniformly reduce in size. Unfortunately the circumferential shrinkage is 4% and this 2% difference causes stress and distortion.

For any particular piece of wood, the amount of distortion depends on how it is cut from the tree. A quarter cut piece of wood has minimum distortion; its thickness reduces by the circumferential shrinkage and its width will reduce by the radial shrinkage. Flat-sawn wood will cup away from the centre. A thin piece of wood will distort more than a thick piece because each section has the freedom to move as it needs. On a thick piece of wood, its bulk restraints the shrinkage/distortion, but then it will have considerable internal stresses. Then, when a thick piece of dry wood is turned relatively thin, the stress restraints are relieved and the remaining wood is now free to move. This is why even dry-turned pieces can distort when finished. It is particularly noticeable on weak shapes, such as large flat platters, and not so apparent on strong shapes, like bowls. This is where the part-turning process comes into play: a bowl is turned over thickness, allowed to dry completely and distort, then returned to the lathe for finishing. Pieces turned in this way should be completely stable.

A moisture meter will help you monitor the condition of the wood. But even without a moisture meter you can calculate when a piece has reached EMC. This is done by weighing the blank at, say, weekly intervals and plotting a graph of weight against time. Weighing the wood will tell you whether it has taken in or lost moisture and then, when the weight does not change, EMC has been reached.

Buying wood

If you buy kiln-dried blanks, then make sure that they are completely sealed so that they cannot take in moisture. It is always very tempting to buy expensive blanks with attractive grain colour and figure, which greatly enhance the final turned piece and make it a more desirable object. And it is certainly true that a fancy grain sells better than a plain one. But a mistake on an expensive piece of wood is an expensive mistake and, when you are learning, it is more likely to happen because the value of the wood gets in the way of your turning development. While learning, use cheap or free wood so that it doesn't matter if you make mistakes when the tool touches the wood. While the equipment will have cost quite a lot of money, it is worth remembering that you could spend just as much, if not more, on wood in the first ten years of turning.

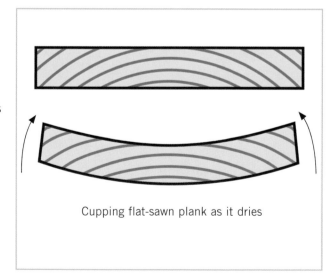

Cupping flat-sawn plank as it dries

Sandpaper

Sandpaper – or, to use the industry term, coated abrasives – are cutting tools, but with the great advantage that they don't have to be sharpened and they will work on any shape and grain direction. They are included at this stage in the book to reflect their importance as essential tools in the turning process.

Coated abrasives consist of three basic materials: abrasive grain, backing and the bond. We use them in three different ways: firstly to refine the shape of the surface, smoothing out any irregularities; secondly to remove any tool marks and rough grain areas; and thirdly, to create a fine, uniform smooth surface, so that when a finish is applied it adheres and penetrates evenly. The importance of this last one was brought home to me when a woodturning friend, Kevin Lightfoot, supplied 300 turned stair spindles to a local joinery firm. The design called for a long straight section in the middle. Kevin got a great finish on this section with the skew chisel and so did not sand it as he had done for the rest of the spindle. All 300 spindles were returned from the joiners for sanding on the centre section; the surface was so smooth that the finish would not adhere to it.

Of course, there are times that the marks left by the tools become part of the piece, so then sanding is not required. There are also dangers in the excessive use of abrasives as they can soften sharp detail, particularly on spindles.

Below Various coated abrasives.

Above Power sanding pads and discs with Velcro fixing.

Types of coated abrasives

Coated abrasives come in various forms: as sheets, the traditional form; on rolls, which are easy to handle and usually more economical; and as discs, which usually have a Velcro backing and are used for power sanding. The grains are arranged on the backing in one of two ways: closed coat, where the abrasive grains cover 100% of the coat side surface of the backing; and open coat, where the individual grains are spaced out. In open coats, about 50–70% of the coated surface is covered with abrasive.

Backing

Paper or cloth backing is measured by weight, which is determined by the tensile strength of the backing.

Paper

The weight and flexibility of paper backings are represented by the letters A–E. A and B are lightweight and highly flexible. C and D weights are medium to heavyweight for more strength and less flexibility. E weight is a strong, durable heavy paper stock coated in a complete range of grit sizes, primarily used for mechanical sanding operations.

Cloth

There are two common types of cloth backings. One is a heavy, strong, relatively stiff material. It is used in coarse grit belts for heavy stock removal on straight or flat surfaces. The other is a lighter, less strong, relatively soft and flexible material known as J weight or jeans cloth. It is used in finishing work or contour work on curved surfaces where finish and uniformity are more important than stock removal.

Bond

Bond is the agent used to hold the abrasive grains onto the backing. It is usually a combination of layers of adhesives. **Resin** is a synthetic adhesive used as a bond. Resins are strong and resist moisture and heat build-up. Glue, which is traditionally made from animal hides, is another type of an adhesive used as a bond. **Make coat** is the initial layer of adhesive into which the abrasive grains are embedded. **Size coat** is the secondary layer of adhesive that covers the majority of the abrasive grains.

What coated abrasive to use

Use garnet and white aluminium oxide for general applications and silver-grey silicon carbide to finish on close-grained dense hardwoods, such as African blackwood. Emery should only be used on very dark woods as the grain can come off and penetrate the wood. Use flexible backings on projects with fine detail so that the abrasive will follow the turned form. At the other extreme, use a strong backing with coarse grits to smooth flat surfaces, such as rolling pins, to remove high spots. Waterproof bonds and backing should be used on green wood and for wet sanding.

Wire wool

Wire wool is made from fine strands of drawn mild steel formed into a pad. Each strand is approximately triangular in section. Its primary use by woodturners is for a final smoothing or polishing of the finished surface, sometimes with the application of a paste wax finish at the same time. Wire wool is graded from 5 to 0000; 5 is coarse and 0000 is very fine.

Below Very fine 0000 grade wire wool.

Finishes

When all the turning is done and the wood surface has been smoothed to a fine and even texture, applying some form of surface finish will bring out the natural beauty of the wood and provide a durable surface coating.

There are many types of finishes for general woodwork, all of which can be used on turned wooden items to good effect. There are many more, instant finishes, designed to meet the particular demands of the woodturner. These are finishes that can be applied on the lathe, friction-dried and buffed; the piece taken from the lathe is then completely finished. There are certainly tens, if not hundreds, of these commercial finishes available. And, without going to the trouble of asking for the data sheets for each product, it is often very difficult to distinguish between them. The name and description on the tin are usually much more about marketing and what the product is intended to achieve – which of course is important – but they often give little indication as to what is in the tin. Not all finishes are compatible with each other, so check the base of finishes before you attempt to combine them.

There are food-safe finishes, which would not cause harm if you ingested them, but be careful – some are described as food safe, but may only be safe after 30 days when all the volatile organic compounds (VOCs) have evaporated. Be sure to follow the manufacturer's instructions and read all the small print. The same applies to toy-safe finishes.

Types of finishes

The information on the following pages provides an introductory guide to finishes. In the main, finishes can be grouped under four main headings, which represent the type of base material of the products: wax, oil, polish and varnish.

Waxes

Pure waxes are solid in form, at room temperature, with a melting point lower than the boiling point of water. Natural waxes are derived from plants or insects; mineral waxes are obtained by oil distillation and synthetic waxes are produced using oil or natural gas.

Below Beeswax.

The standard test to measure the hardness of wax is called a penetration test. This meaures the depth, in tenths of a millimetre (dmm), that a specially configured and weighted needle will penetrate the wax at certain temperatures. A hard wax would have a low penetration number.

Beeswax A glandular secretion from young worker honeybees for building their honeycomb structures. It is soft, yellow in colour and produces a dull sheen. Hardness of 20dmm at 25°C; melting point 64°C.

Carnauba A wax derived from the leaves of the Brazilian carnauba palm. It is very hard, with high gloss. Hardness 2dmm at 25°C; melting point 84°C.

Paraffin wax This wax is distilled from crude oil. It is a colourless, odourless fatty substance, which produces a soft dull sheen. Paraffin waxes impart high resistance to moisture, alcohol, acids and fingerprints. Hardness greater than 11dmm at 25°C; melting point 75°C.

Polyethylene wax A synthetic wax produced by the polymerization of ethylene. Ethylene is produced from natural gas or by cracking petroleum naphtha. Melts between 30 and 140°C depending on grade. Hardness between 7 and 12dmm at 25°C. Polyethylene waxes increase abrasion resistance and provide a non-sticky wax surface.

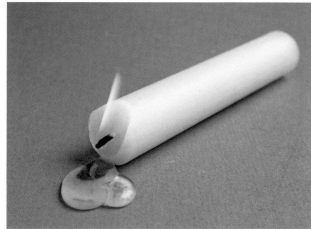

Above Paraffin wax.

Top left Carnauba wax flakes.

Left Carnauba wax block.

Above Sorby paste wax.

Above Liberon Black Bison fine paste wax.

Waxes can also be mixed to give a combination of their properties. **Paste wax** – either pure wax or a blend of waxes in a solvent – is a soft wax produced for ease of application. When applied, the solvent evaporates leaving the hard wax on the surface. With a high level of solvent the mixture becomes a liquid wax. Various solvents are used, such as turpentine, meths and white spirits.

A wax and oil mixture combines the properties of both in liquid form. The oil penetrates the wood, while the wax migrates to the surface and hardens.

Oils

Oils are naturally in liquid form at room temperature. The majority of the oils used for wood finishing are 'drying oils' derived from vegetable origins. The drying is a chemical reaction with oxygen, which changes the oil from a liquid to a solid state. This process is called polymerization. Some oils are pre-polymerized in the manufacturing process to improve drying time and surface hardness. Oils can also be blended with other additives to further improve properties such as drying time, hardness and sheen. The oils are dissolved in a solvent. Every manufacturer has their own recipe.

Natural oils

Natural oils are those derived from the seeds of plants, such as lemon oil, which is derived from the seed of lemongrass and sunflower oil (made from sunflower seed).

Linseed oil is derived from the seed of the flax plant (whose fibre is used for making linen) and it is a drying oil. After the impurities are removed, the oil is polymerized in order to accelerate its drying properties. Mix raw linseed oil with turpentine, for ease of application. Boiled linseed oil, produced by passing hot air through raw linseed oil, has an even faster drying time.

Tung oil is derived from the seed of several species of aleurites and it is polymerized to create a tough waterproof glossy coat. **Danish oil** is a moderately polymerized tung oil, which produces a beautiful satin sheen. **Teak oil** is a blend of tung oil, resins and dryers.

Cooking oils can be used on wood, particularly on items that will be in contact with food. However, their drying properties are not a consideration in manufacture and some oils may go rancid. It would be advisable to test a particular oil to see how it performs.

Mineral oils

Liquid paraffin is a transparent, colourless, almost odourless oily liquid composed of saturated hydrocarbons, which are obtained by distillation from petroleum. This is a non-drying oil but it fills the cells in the wood and leaves a waterproof protective film on the surface. It is also food safe out of the bottle. It may adhere to fatty foods but is otherwise a nice finish.

Polishes

Polish is shellac dissolved in a solvent; usually methylated spirits. When applied to wood, the solvent evaporates, leaving the shellac on the surface. Shellac is the resinous excreta of the lac beetle. It is solid in its natural form, dissolves readily in ethanol (methylated spirits) and can be used in a variety of ways. It is harder and more durable than waxes but as its melting point is lower than the boiling point of water, it is susceptible to heat damage.

Shellac is available in many forms: bleached; button polish; French polish; button shellac; blond; ultra blond; blond dewax shellac; granulated white lac; and golden or orange flake shellac. The most readily available and versatile of these is the golden or orange flake shellac, also known as SILTN. **French polish** is applied manually by 'padding' it onto the surface. **Friction polish** is similar to French polish, but is formulated to dry quickly on the lathe by the application of a polishing cloth to create heat.

Varnish and lacquer

In its most basic form varnish is made up of a binder that is naturally solid at room temperature, dissolved (or suspended) in a solvent. The binder is either resin, lacquer or cellulose. When applied to wood the solvent evaporates, leaving the binder on the surface.

Resin and lacquer

Resins and lacquers are solid (or semi-solid) amorphous substances exuded from certain trees, primarily the lacquer tree. Slower-drying natural lacquers contain oleoresins.

Above Shellac button polish.

Above Left to right: Liberon Danish oil; Liberon finishing oil; Sorby friction polish; Sorby Danish oil; boiled linseed oil; organ burnishing oil; organ finishing oil; Sorby universal lacquer; Sorby lemon oil; liquid paraffin.

Cellulose

Cellulose is carbohydrate, a starchy substance that forms the cell walls of plants. Cellulose derived from the cotton plant and treated with nitric and sulphuric acid makes nitrocellulose (cellulose nitrate), which is the primary resin material used in making cellulose lacquer. The solvent used in cellulose lacquer is not compatible with other solvents. Cellulose-based lacquers are harder and more chemical resistant than other resin-based lacquers.

Synthetic

Synthetic varnishes are usually organic; they have a polymeric structure produced by synthetically composing molecules. Modern technology has developed synthetic varnishes that have a very similar molecular structure to natural lacquer.

Acrylic

Acrylic varnishes are made up of synthetic resin suspended in water. It is the use of water that distinguishes acrylics from other varnishes because there is no use of volatile organic compounds (VOCs), which are harmful to both the individual and the environment. Acrylics are faster drying than solvent-borne resins and are also generally tougher than solvent-dissolved resins.

Commercial products

Varnish and lacquer can be a mixture of resin and polymerizing oil in a solvent. The solvent evaporates with the resin and the oil polymerizes, leaving a hard and dry coating on the wood. The use of additives further improves its drying and wearing qualities.

Craftlac melamine is a cellulose-based finish. It contains melamine particles and toluene solvent, which produces a tough finish. Use cellulose thinners with this product.

Sanding sealers are varnishes (resin, cellulose or acrylic-based) with wood dust added. The purpose is to fill and seal the pores of wood with the wood particles, creating a clean, smooth surface when the surface varnish is sanded off. The wood dust is usually made from white wood so beware of using it on open-grained dark woods. Sanding sealers are usually used as preparation before another finish.

The workshop

It goes without saying that we need a dedicated space for turning. I would normally call this space a workshop, but then I have met one turner who manages to turn in the house and another who turns in the attic!

A shed at the bottom of the garden or part of the garage are more likely venues. Few turners have the luxury of a purpose-built workshop but, whatever the size of the work space, careful planning of its layout will make a big difference to the turning experience. The biggest problem for the woodturner is a workshop that looks fine before the turning starts, but becomes a nightmare afterwards when it comes to looking for that tool buried under a pile of shavings.

Dedicated areas

Grouping pieces of equipment that are used for the same process allows an easy workflow through the work space, effectively dividing up the working area – this can be anything from a line on the floor to a solid wall. I would suggest dedicating areas for turning; special equipment; general working; wood storage and spraying.

Below My neighbour Michael Barnett's workshop with good access for taking in timber and removing shavings.

62

Turning area

This is one area that I would partition physically. The simplest, most effective method is to use cheap and easily movable strips of heavy plastic sheet (similar to industrial drive-through doors). This will help to contain the wood-shavings in a small area around the lathe and protect other equipment from becoming covered in shavings.

Dust extraction should become more efficient because the air flow is directed. The plastic strips let the light through, are no barrier to movement and can be easily moved when not required. You could also make them informative or decorative by printing on them.

In the turning area put the lathe, a grinder, a rack for the turning tools, a drawered cabinet to store the chucks and other hand tools and possibly a workbench. Ensure you have enough storage so that surfaces can be left clear.

One of the biggest, dirtiest, unhealthiest and probably the most hated jobs for a woodturner is cleaning up wood-shavings and dust. The fewer tools, timber and equipment there are to get covered in dust and shavings, the easier the working and cleaning becomes. A large external door on the turning area makes for easy disposal of the wood-shavings. Perhaps you may want to include the bandsaw in the turning area because, like the lathe, it creates a lot of dust, shavings and off-cuts. But a few years ago I moved my bandsaw outdoors, to give me more room for a project I was working on, with the intention of moving it back when the project was finished. However, I loved using the bandsaw outside in the fresh air and the dust and off-cuts were much easier to deal with. I also loved the improvement to the workshop environment and consequently, the bandsaw did not go back. Yes, there were days when I couldn't use it because of the weather (even in Scotland) but this was far offset by the advantages. I made up a sack-type cover from a tarpaulin for weather protection and used a circuit breaker on the power supply for electrical safety. My bandsaw has now moved to another building that is only used for rough cutting wood.

Above My double-bag chip extractor and compressor in separate shed.

Special equipment area

It might seem logical to have the dust extractor in the turning section. But they are very noisy, take up valuable space and, if you have the old-fashioned, double-bag style, then they will certainly recirculate the finest dust, which is dangerous. Even an efficient extractor that removes particles down to 5 microns may still recirculate any finer dust.

The best place for the dust extractor is in a small equipment shed or box adjacent to the workshop, with a large suction pipe into the turning area. A remote switch with a pull string above the lathe will make it very convenient to switch it on and off and, being out of the workshop, it will be quieter so there should be no problem having it running most of the time. Fit a suction funnel that is designed to suck a wide area and can be easily moved to where the dust is being generated. Because the air and dust are not recirculated, I think this is a more efficient set-up than having a longer suction pipe.

Above Store green wood outside.

Above Ensure there are gaps to permit airflow.

Compressed air in the workshop is a great boon for power tools, spraying and cleaning up, especially on all the shelves and awkward corners. Again, a compressor is a noisy piece of equipment so if possible put it in the equipment shed with the dust extractor and run an airline into the workshop. I also store my chainsaws in the special equipment area.

General working area

Any other tools that are not needed in the turning process, along with the machinery workbench and DIY finishes, can go in the general working area. This will be a nice place to work once the turning area is sectioned off.

Storing timber

Whatever condition your timber arrives in, it is unlikely to remain in the same state unless it is stored in a suitable place. Green wood stored in somewhere warm will quickly start to dry and almost certainly crack. Kiln-dried wood stored in a damp, humid area will start to take in moisture and eventually have the same moisture content as air-dried timber; therefore the money spent on drying will have been wasted. Storing green wood and kiln-dried wood together will be good for neither of them.

If the workshop is heated and warm, then there should be no problem storing dry timber and maintaining its moisture content. Store dry wood in the warmest part of the workshop and, if possible,

provide some warm air circulation. In addition, kiln-dried blanks should be coated with a wax or similar barrier to prevent moisture ingress. But as many workshops are unheated and cold most of the time (well, certainly in Scotland!), then storing small amounts of dry wood in a warm corner of the house could be an ideal solution.

Part-turned items from green wood require a cool, dry location with good air circulation to bring down the moisture content before they are transferred to a dryer area. Store green timber in the round outdoors, protected from the weather, but with good air circulation. Lay it on a hard, dry surface.

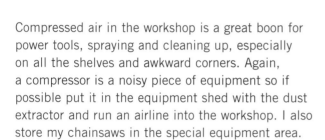

Left Make sure your wood is stored properly.

Right It's a good idea to mark your timber.

Left
My workshop.

Spraying

The workshop is not a safe place to spray. The particles will remain in the atmosphere long after you have taken the protective gear off. If spraying is a regular part of your process, then a spray booth will be essential. For occasional spraying find somewhere other than the workshop area. I live in the countryside and spray just outside the workshop.

Workshop layout
Lathe position

It might seem tempting to put the lathe up against the wall, where it appears to take up the least amount of space. In my opinion this is the worst possible position because it can feel confined standing close to the wall and a tool rack or shelves on the wall exacerbates the problem. It is difficult to organize good lighting and it can also restrict tool movement for some bowl projects, although a swivel head lathe could alleviate this. I sometimes work from the other side of the lathe and there is nothing worse than trying to clean around a lathe that is next to the wall. A good position is one where you stand between the wall and the lathe; the wall can then be used for tool racks and shelves for chucks. But placing the lathe at 90º to the wall could restrict either using the outboard end or long-hole boring, depending on its position.

However, if it is essential to keep the lathe against the wall when it is not being used, then make it movable and add lockable castors, which will provide flexibility in all situations. I now have a small, cam-operated trolley on castors underneath my Vicmarc lathe, which makes moving it a simple operation.

Tools

Most tools should be stored on easily accessible wall racks, but when it comes to using them on projects, it is very handy to have those tools and abrasives needed on a surface close to the lathe. A good solution is to have a movable or swinging shelf by the tailstock on which to store tools for that particular job. When the shelf is not required it can be moved to a more suitable position. A movable trolley is also ideal. It is not ideal to keep the tools on the lathe bed, or even on a shelf under the lathe bed, because they will get covered in wood shavings and may also be knocked off.

Grinder position

I sharpen my tools every few minutes – they have to be really sharp for turning green wood – and in those few minutes I remove an awful lot of wood. This means that the grinder should be close to the lathe so that I hardly need to move my feet for a quick grind, then back to turning. I like to position the grinder at the tailstock end of the lathe.

Power points

There are a number of situations when you will use other power tools in connection with the lathe, such as power sanding, fluting with a router, drilling and so on. To operate these you will need a number of power points close by. I like to have them above the lathe at the tailstock end so that they are easily accessible and the cables are not trailing on the floor. If you use air, place an air point next to the electrical points to give you a choice of power supply.

Lighting

You need good general lighting in the workshop. Natural lighting is best, which requires plenty of windows, Roof lights are effective and give a nicer

light. You will also need good artificial lighting. Fluorescents are relatively economical but there is the possibility of a strobe effect, which can be dangerous for lathe work. It is not a problem I have personally experienced, but beware if you do use them. If you only have one light in the middle of the workshop there is a 90% chance that your back will be to the light. It is better to have lights at either side of the workshop – about a quarter of the workshop width in from the wall. This will give a more even light distribution throughout, although it is always worth making special adjustments for equipment and machinery in the workshop.

In addition you will need good local lighting to cast light on any particular area of the piece being turned. This is best provided by a movable light. Ease of movement and a good range is important as you don't want to be struggling with it – I have seen many a light ruin a good piece of work. Most lathes do not provide a suitable location for fixing a light, although the accessory bar on the One Way lathe is an exception. If you can make up something similar, you will appreciate the ease with which your lighting can be adjusted.

Below Tools on a portable rack.

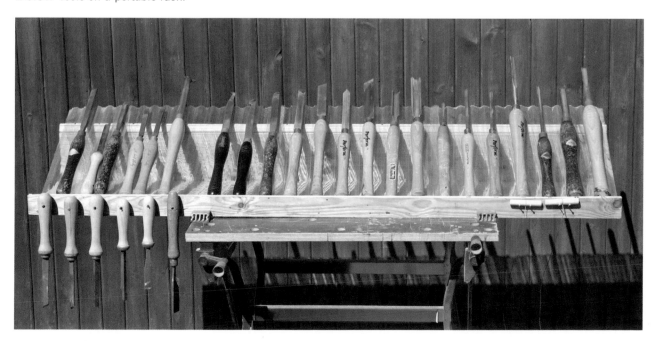

Part two – Techniques

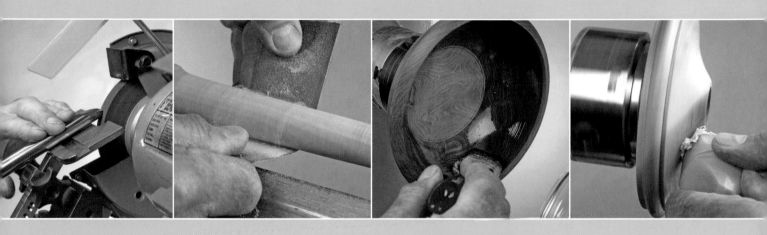

When you, the turner, take a tool in your hands you become one. Hopefully, you are moving together, applying pressure so that the keen edge of the tool cuts the wood with fine control to make the desired shape. Getting this right is to combine all the aspects of turning in a series of movements that will guide the tool through the wood, repeating them over and over again until the finished piece appears. This section looks at the individual aspects that a turner needs to consider when preparing for and making a cut on the lathe.

Safety

We tend to call accidents, accidents, as if we had nothing to do with the event and it was beyond our control. But if you take reasonable precautions then the majority of so-called accidents can be avoided.

Always keep a powder fire extinguisher in the workshop.

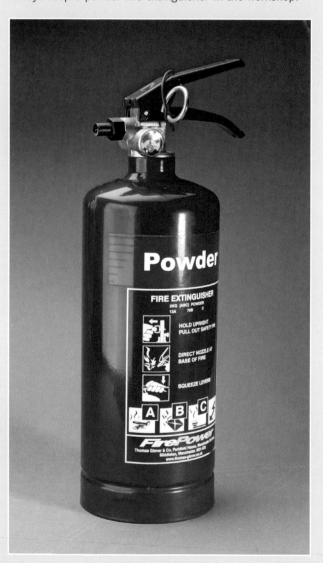

The most obvious danger is coming into contact with bandsaws, chainsaws and circular saws, grinders, rotating pieces of wood and sharp tools. But there are two other, insidious dangers, that don't cause pain or immediate effect. These are noise and dust. The effects of both are cumulative and long term, reducing both quality and even length of life. I do have a few scars from sharp edges of tools, the significance of which became negligible a few weeks after the event. But the asthma, for which I have regular medication; the loss of hearing and tinnitus, which I have had for years, will only get worse. And these are probably down to woodturning.

Safety has to be something we do naturally as part of our normal routine. If safety causes inconvenience or even expense, then there is always a tendency to ignore it. But when it comes to woodturning, safety and efficient working practices have more in common than you might think. For example, when sharpening my tools I stand to the side of the grinder so that I am close to the action, with a good view of the sharpening and good tool control. From a safety point of view I am no longer in line with the sparks generated and if a wheel did break, I am not in the main danger area (although I have never known a wheel to break). If you do much the same when turning you are not as likely to get covered in shavings or be in line with the wood, if it should unfortunately come out of the lathe. So 'thinking' safety can improve your working practices.

Primary safety

I have what I call 'primary safety' and 'secondary safety'. Primary safety is the avoidance of danger and staying away, such as standing to one side when switching on the lathe for the first time with a new piece of wood. Secondary safety is the addition of safety equipment, whether it be personal protection or in the workshop. Personally, I try to achieve primary safety whenever possible: I turn green wood to minimize dust (and it is much more fun than turning dry wood).

Dos and Don'ts

Do

Make sure that manufacturers' safety equipment is correctly fitted to all machinery.

Keep the noise down. Machinery is noisy and can make the workshop uncomfortable, so keep noise down by having as much as possible of machinery outside the workroom or wear ear protectors.

Minimize the dust in the atmosphere by having a dust extraction system which does not recirculate fine dust. If possible, place the dust extractor outside the workshop to reduce dust and noise.

Don't

Be messy! A workshop that is tidy and well-organized is a safer working environment. It is also easier to find things when they're not covered in shavings

Don't forget to have all the appropriatthe equipment handy so it is easy to use.

Don't forget your ear muffs.

My dust extractor is outside the workshop to reduce noise and dust, and I always keep my workshop clean and well-organized.

A warm workshop is a comfortable environment in which to work and this can also reduce the risk of accidents, but not if the heat comes from a wood-shavings stove! These are likely to get covered in shavings and I know of two turners' workshops that have burnt down.

Accidents do happen

Even if after taking all necessary precautions, you do have an accident, be prepared to deal with the consequences. Keep a first aid kit handy; even some first aid training would not go amiss. Keep a suitable fire extinguisher by the exit or better still, in an adjacent shed. Don't forget that they need regular maintenance and validating. Keep a telephone handy to call for help. And if all else fails, have a good insurance policy.

First aid kit.

Safety equipment

Safety equipment might not be on your mind when you are buying a lathe and woodturning tools, but it should be. It is essential to purchase safety equipment at the same time – accidents won't wait to happen.

Right Record Power drum dust extractor, capable of filtering down to 5 microns.

Below Record double-bag dust extractor, fitted with a filter to collect fine particles.

Dust extraction

Whatever kind of wood you are using, a dust extractor is a must – the more powerful the better. However, watch the noise level if the dust extractor is going to be in the workshop. Not only will it create another hazard, a noisy dust extractor will be switched off at the earliest convenience, or more likely not switched on at all. Dust extractors should be able to collect dust down to 5 microns. Old double-bag type extractors may not be capable of this and will recirculate the fine, dangerous dust. These should only be used as dust extractors if they are outside the workshop. In addition, it could be worth having a smaller filter in the workshop that can be left running to clear the atmosphere of the finest dust.

Chainsaw safety

This is a particular situation for which there is specialist safety equipment from full head gear and specially padded clothing that will clog the chain to gloves and steel toe-capped boots. It is always worth taking a course on chainsaw use and safety.

Right Ivor Thomas wearing safety boots, leggings, gloves and helmet with ear muffs and face shield.

Personal protection

Your safety gear should be comfortable, easy to put on and take off and must not impede the production, otherwise it will just be left on the shelf.

A minimum requirement for protecting your eyes should be a pair of goggles that also give some protection at the sides. A full face shield gives better face protection but can mist up, which restricts visibility. A simple dust mask can be very effective, but make sure it fits well and that there are no leakage points. Avoid heavy or bulky masks, which restrict visibility and sometimes cause condensation in the mouth piece. Masks that provide a combination of eye and respiratory protection are a more expensive option but can be a good investment. They provide better protection and are often easier to use. There are two types. The compact has the motor and batteries in the helmet. This is heavier on the head but is ideal for recreational use. The other type has the battery and motor on a belt with a hose to the helmet. This is usually more powerful and ideal for professional use. Whichever type you choose, make sure you keep the batteries charged.

Finally, most machinery is noisy, so a good pair of ear protectors is essential.

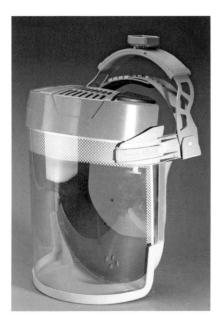

Left Racal dust master helmet.

Left Racal AirFlow helmet. A compact battery and motor is contained within the helmet.

Approaching the lathe

There was a time when 'one size fits all' socks filled the shelves, which was fine for those people in the middle of the size range, but for people like me, shoe size 12, it was always a struggle pulling them on as my feet were often beyond the stretch limit of the socks. And what about the guy at the other end of the range, walking around with the heels halfway up his leg? But things are much better now – there are socks available in my size, which is very nice.

Below left Checking lathe height for turning with the deep-fluted gouge.

Below middle Checking grinder height sharpening spindle roughing gouge.

Below right Roughing a spindle, controlling the gouge with my left hand.

Height

Lathes are a bit like clothes – they have to 'fit' the turner to get the best out of them. A lathe has a fixed height and you probably don't even think about it. However, it can make an enormous difference to your ability to turn. If it is too low then you have to stoop over the lathe; too high, and you don't have the manoeuvrability or power behind the tool. These problems can be solved by either raising the height of the lathe, or increasing your height, which is easy enough.

It's simple enough to find out the ideal lathe centre height for you. Take one of your spindle turning tools, such as the spindle roughing gouge, turn your back on the lathe, then pretend to rough down a spindle in what you feel is a comfortable position. Remain in that position and measure the height (or better still, get someone else to), from the ground to the tool, about 1in (25mm) from the cutting edge. This should be the tool rest height, which is close enough to the lathe spindle height that you will need for spindle turning.

But I have found that I need a different lathe height for bowl turning than for spindle turning. Do the same exercise again, this time with the deep-fluted gouge, and pretend to turn the outside of a bowl. This is more of a 'power cut', with the tool positioned to deliver the power; in my case the measurement was 3in (75mm) lower. I have different lathes for spindle and bowl turning, but if you use the same lathe for both, set the lathe up to its highest position, then use duckboards to raise and lower yourself (or anyone else using the lathe). This will help you achieve optimum working height. A little bit of latitude in height won't matter too much as the height of the tool rest can be fine-tuned for any given tool. In total, I raised my Graduate bowl-turning lathe by 6in (152mm) and my Graduate spindle-turning lathe by 8in (203mm).

Tool rest height

Adjusting the tool rest height will set the presentation angle for particular tools and determine just how comfortable it is to use. Too high and it will be tight; too low and you can hardly reach the handle. For most tools, a comfortable working angle is between the horizontal and 30° below. The scraper is an exception as it is used above the horizontal to achieve a trailing cut.

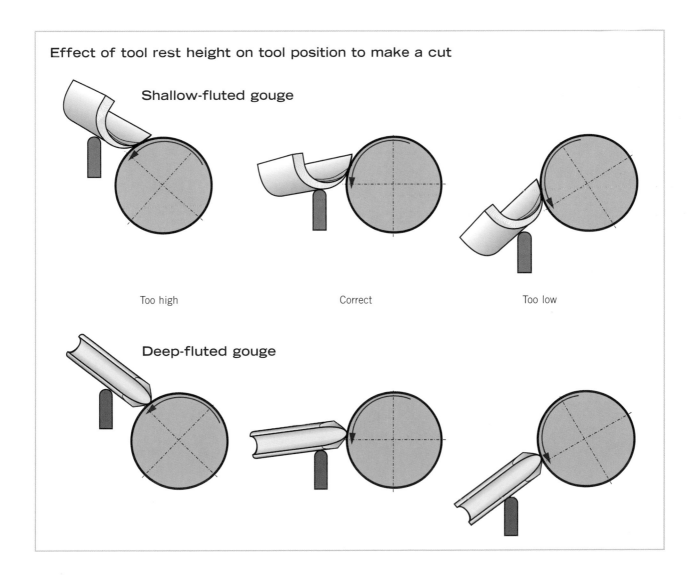

Effect of tool rest height on tool position to make a cut

Shallow-fluted gouge

Too high   Correct   Too low

Deep-fluted gouge

Above A dynamic stance for tool sharpening, standing to the side of the high-speed grinder.

Tool sharpening equipment

The height of the tool sharpening equipment will also need adjusting. High-speed grinders are generally called bench grinders, but a bench is the last place to put one because it would be far too low for effective and comfortable use. Again, the way to find the optimum working height is to pretend to sharpen a tool, then measure the height of the tool from the ground, about 1in (25mm) from the end. This will be the grinder axis height, or the height of the platform on the Sorby belt sharpening system. In my case, this is 4in (102mm) higher than the spindle turning lathe axis height of 42in (1067mm).

If you use a wetstone grinder then follow the same procedure. You are likely to be working on the top of the wheel so that the water runs back onto the wheel. Hold the tool in a comfortable position and pretend to sharpen. Measure the height of the tool tip to give you the tool rest height (or the height of the top of the wheel). For me, this is about 20in (508mm) lower than the spindle on the high-speed grinder.

Right Comfortable height and stance for tool sharpening on the Sorby belt sharpening system.

Above Comfortable height and stance for tool sharpening on the top of the Tormek wetstone grinder.

Sharpening height

	High-speed grinder	Wetstone grinder
Deep-fluted gouge	45in+ (1143mm)	50in (1270mm)
Spindle roughing gouge	48in (1219mm)	50½in (1283mm)
Shallow-fluted gouge	49½in (1232mm)	50in (1270mm)

Stance

Look at people standing in a bus queue, particularly at their feet, which will probably be about 8in (203mm) apart, with the toes pointing out slightly and legs fairly straight. This is a 'static stance', which is relaxed and physically inactive – ideal when waiting for the bus. Then look at someone like a boxer or fencer in action. Their stance is entirely different, with one foot well in front of the other, knees bent and constantly moving. This is a 'dynamic stance', which has power, movement and agility. A joiner will take a dynamic stance when planing a piece of wood, with one foot well in front of the other, in-line with the cut to be made. This allows the joiner to apply the force evenly all the way along the wood.

Above A typical 'waiting for the bus' stance.

Left Static stance – feet close together.

I once had a very beautiful gouge, which was forged, very shallow, about 1¼in (32mm) wide and sharpened with a long fingernail grind. I never used it for fear of losing its beautiful bevel, which had probably last been sharpened in the 1920s or 30s. This gouge had puzzled me as I could not see how the turner would make full use of the large fingernail cutting edge. This was until another turner pointed out the user was probably standing on one leg – in other words, working on a treadle or pole lathe. The turner would make lots of fine cuts because of the limited power. He would probably make the cuts towards himself, a direction in which he would be most stable and able to apply the force and movement to make the cut. Putting the gouge in its correct historical context brought it to life.

The lathes we use now have powerful electric motors up to 3hp (2.5kW). Electronic variable speed means that the belts don't even need to be changed and the speed can be adjusted as the project progresses. Turning tools are now bigger, longer and stronger, allowing turners to take advantage of the great power available. With these developments, you are free from the restraint of having to provide the power to drive the lathe and can take a suitable stance for the job. A dynamic stance will give you the power and agility to make and control the cut. Standing with feet slightly apart sideways and one foot well in front of the other, the turner can apply forward pressure along the tool to cut the wood, while allowing sideways movement swinging the tool around curves.

Tip
A good lathe should have space for your knees and toes so that you can stand and work comfortably. A bad lathe would be one which is mounted on a flat-fronted bench that doesn't have a toe kick space. Toes and knees have nowhere to go, which will greatly affect the turning and can cause back problems. If the lathe is set back from the front edge then this exacerbates the problem. If you can put your toe (and possibly your knee) up to the centre line under the lathe, then you should be fine.

Above Ready for action.

Left Dynamic stance – feet apart for power and agility.

78

Above Turning the outside of a cross-grain bowl left-handed.

Top Turning the outside of a cross-grain bowl left-handed on the Harrison short bed.

Woodturning

Take up the correct stance while approaching the lathe, having already mounted the blank and set up the tool rest position. Stand back from the lathe, take a deep-fluted gouge in any hand, place it on the tool rest and line up the bevel with the direction of cut. Stand behind the tool, looking down the bevel in the direction of cut, change hands if necessary, then take a dynamic stance, ready to make a cut away from yourself. In this position you will have very good control over the cut and the wood-shavings will be directed away from you. You will also be in the safest position should the wood leave the lathe. This can mean working from the opposite side of the lathe and occasionally I even sit on the lathe in order to get myself in the best position to turn. A swivel head lathe would avoid having to do this.

Now I reckon that when you initially make this approach to the lathe, about 30% of the time you will find that the handle does not fall into your natural hand. This is when you will find out that you need to be ambidextrous to be a good turner. It might feel a little strange at first but it will quickly become natural and greatly improve your woodturning technique. Of course, there are exceptions when doing fine detail work, such as vees, beads and coves, or very small items. It would be silly to change hands to do the opposite side of a bead or cove – it could slow the job down and the result might not be as good. But even with these detail cuts, a dynamic stance is needed. Stand behind the tool for the initial cut, which effectively means to the side of it. I usually take the most dynamic stance for the finest cuts.

Right A dynamic stance, to the side of the grinder brings you close to the action while being in the safest place.

Above Turning inside a bowl right-handed.

Tool sharpening

A good stance can make a great difference to tool sharpening. If you are using a high-speed grinder, standing to the side brings you close to the action with a very good view of the sharpening process. You are also out of the way of sparks. A dynamic stance makes the process easier and quicker. Follow the same rule as when turning fine details: hold the handle in your natural hand, which will dictate on what side of the grinder you stand.

Sawing

When it comes to putting wood through a saw, be it a circular saw or bandsaw, your stance should be a safety issue. Taking a static stance can be dangerous. For instance, if the wood moved forward suddenly, through a soft spot in the wood or similar, and you were to fall forward, then the teeth of the saw would be very close to the fingers. Good practice and safety are in tune with each other.

Holding the tool

How you hold the tool is the final part of controlling the turning process. One hand should hold the handle while the other holds the stock. Which hand you use to hold the tool will depend on the cut you make, as well as your preference for left- or right-handedness. There are a number of different grips for each hand, which also depend on the cut being made. The grip can vary at different stages through the cut.

The control hand is the one that holds the handle; it provides most of the force and the movement required to make cuts and create shapes. The hand holding the stock is the support hand; this should fine-tune the cut, while keeping the tool firmly on the rest and holding the bevel against the wood. It can pull or push the tool as required.

Control hand

For the control hand, there are two grips:

Power grip

Hold the end of the handle with the fingers wrapped round the handle and the thumb running along the top, pointing to the stock. The thumb on top gives more flexibility of movement than with the thumb wrapped round. This grip is used when removing lots of wood on large simple shapes, straight lines and large curves, where there is little or no twisting needed to make the cut.

Variation: The control hand is held against the hip for extra power and stability.

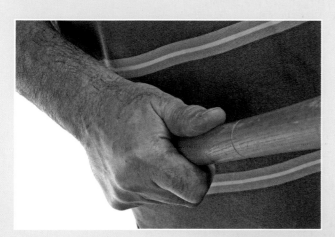

Flexi grip

The narrowest part of the handle is held between the fingertips and thumb. In this grip the tool can easily be rotated. This is for delicate detailed work, where the tool has to be twisted to cut shapes such as beads and coves.

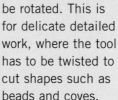

Top left Control hand. Power grip with the DFG.

Left Control hand. Flexi grip with DFG.

Right Support hand. Fingers grip with the skew chisel.

Below right Control hand. Fingers grip with the SFG, heel of hand on rest.

Support hand

For the support hand there are five grips, with variations.

Fingers The simplest grip is with straight fingers resting on top of the stock, so the hand does not touch the tool rest. In this position the tool is held firmly on the rest and the fingers can either push or pull the tool, and hold the bevel against the wood. This grip can be used on long sweeping cuts with the DFG, SRG or skew chisel.

Variation: If the cut is a short one, or a direct entry is being made, the heel of the hand can be fixed on the tool rest (as if it were glued), while the fingers are placed on top of the tool to move it backwards and forward.

Back grip Here, the stock is held underhand (the hand under the tool) between fingertips and thumb. The thumb is behind or on top, fingers in front, hand not touching the tool rest. This grip is used for large, simple shapes, such as using the DFG on a bowl or the SRG to rough a long spindle.

Variation: The back of the hand is placed against the rest (again, as if it were glued). The tool, held between fingers and thumb, can easily be pushed, pulled or twisted to make short cuts. This grip is used for detail cuts.

Above right Support hand. Back grip with the DFG.

Right Support hand. Back grip with the SRG, gouge supported on rest.

Left Support hand. Hook grip with the skew chisel.

Below left Support hand. Thumbs up grip with the SFG, supported on rest.

Hook grip The index finger is hooked under the tool rest with the stock held between fingers and thumb. There is a tension between the index finger and the fingers holding the stock, pulling the tool down onto the rest. This gives good flexibility for fine control on detail cuts.

Thumbs up The back of the fingers are against the tool rest (not touching tool), with thumb on top of the tool. The tool is pressed on the rest while it is pushed and pulled.
   Variation: For bowl rim support, the thumb is placed on top of the stock while the fingers can support the thin bowl wall. The side of hand is on the tool rest.

Over hand grip A particular grip for sheer scraping cuts, the forearm is laid in the tool rest and can slide along it. The tool is gripped with the fingers (not the hand), full around the stock, with thumb on stock (a mirror image of the flexi grip). The movement becomes a whole body movement as the tool is slid backwards and forward across the wood.

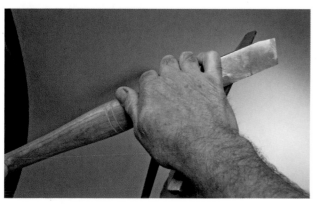

Above left Support hand. Thumbs up grip with the DFG, finger support to the wood.

Left Support hand. Overhand grip for shear scraping.

Entering the wood

The first point of contact between the cutting edge and the wood is the most important part of the cut. A smooth entry leads to a nice flow into the wood, creating the shape. Indeed it defines the rest of the cut. The first action is to set the tool rest position.

Tool rest position

There needs to be a gap of about ½in (13mm) between the tool rest and the wood before the first cut. Any less and the tool bevel could be sitting on the rest, or the tool will make contact with the wood before you are ready. The gap gives you time to set up the cut and make a controlled entry into the wood.

Entering the wood

There are three ways in which I make the first contact between tool and wood: supported entry, direct entry and floating entry. The method I use depends on the cut being made.

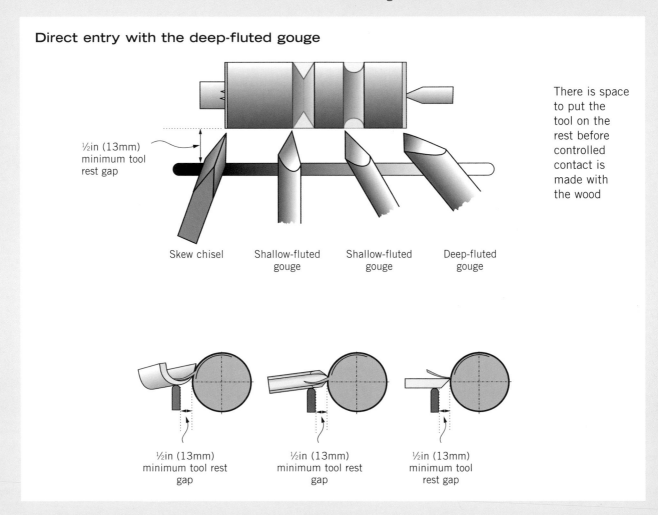

Direct entry with the deep-fluted gouge

½in (13mm) minimum tool rest gap

Skew chisel

Shallow-fluted gouge

Shallow-fluted gouge

Deep-fluted gouge

There is space to put the tool on the rest before controlled contact is made with the wood

½in (13mm) minimum tool rest gap

½in (13mm) minimum tool rest gap

½in (13mm) minimum tool rest gap

Supported entry A supported entry is one where the first contact between the tool and the wood is with the bevel. This provides support and stability for the tool as the cutting edge is brought into contact with the wood. A supported entry is used where there is a smooth transition along the wood surface.

Typically using the spindle roughing gouge for roughing down a square, a branch or a rough spindle to a cylinder, the bevel heel is brought into contact with the wood, then the tool is slowly slid down the rotating wood until the cutting edge makes contact and the shavings jump off. The tool is then slid from side to side to make the cut.

A supported entry is also used with a skew chisel or shallow-fluted gouge to make a smoothing cut, which starts along the wood surface. Bevel contact is made, then the tool is rolled until it makes contact with the edge to produce a shaving. Then the tool is slid along the surface to make the cut. The same entry is made for the DFG when blending in along a surface.

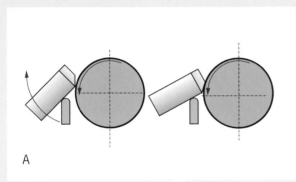

A

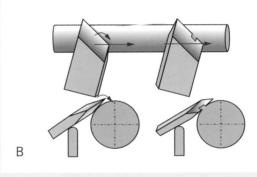

B

A Roughing with the spindle roughing gouge. Heel contact first below the cutting edge, tool handle raised until cutting edge just raises a shaving.

B Skew chisel. The edge of bevel makes contact first, then the skew chisel is rotated until it raises a shaving.

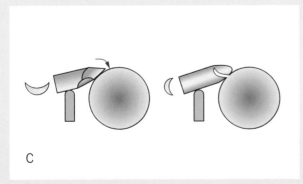

C

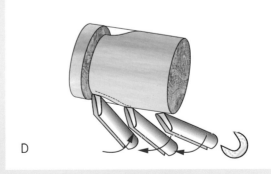

D

C Shallow-fluted gouge being rolled on the bevel until the edge makes contact.

D Shaping with the deep-fluted gouge. Heel contact behind the cutting edge. The handle is swung forward as the tool moves forward, until a shaving is raised. The principle is the same for the shallow-fluted gouge and chisels.

Direct entry A direct entry is one where the first contact between the tool and the wood is the cutting edge. The bevel is lined up with the direction of cut and the tool is slid forward until contact is made. Then, with continued pushing, the cutting edge penetrates the wood and the bevel makes contact with the cut surface, providing support and directional stability for the tool.

This is typically the entry to make when there is a distinct change of surface direction and you want to keep sharp detail. This could be using the DFG to turn a bowl, when the cut starts at the rim, making vees, spigots or squaring off the rim or base. Use this kind of entry also when making chamfers, squaring the end of a spindle with a skew chisel or shallow-fluted gouge and cutting coves – also with a shallow-fluted gouge. When the cutting edge initially makes contact with the wood there is no bevel support – this should be provided by the support hand, with firm grip against the tool rest and holding the tool. Once bevel contact is made, hand support can be reduced.

Making a direct entry

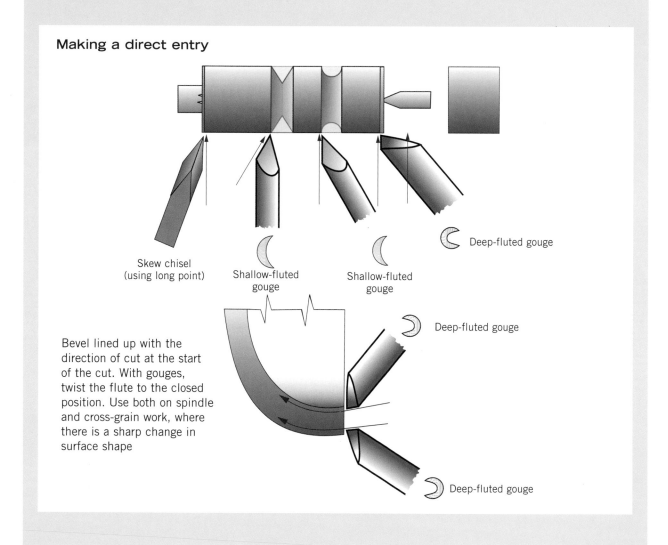

Skew chisel (using long point)

Shallow-fluted gouge

Shallow-fluted gouge

Deep-fluted gouge

Deep-fluted gouge

Deep-fluted gouge

Bevel lined up with the direction of cut at the start of the cut. With gouges, twist the flute to the closed position. Use both on spindle and cross-grain work, where there is a sharp change in surface shape

Floating entry Floating entry is one where the cutting edge is the first point of the tool to touch the wood but there is no bevel contact to follow, such as when using a scraping action with any tool. The edge should glide onto the wood, making contact on the move with the lightest pressure and sliding across the surface (a bit like an aircraft coming in to land). The hand should be sitting on the tool rest, holding the tool firmly but lightly, with a fingers grip. It should be the same whether making a regular scraping cut, with the tool flat on the tool rest, or making a sheer scraping cut.

Entry technique

The tool entry into the wood is the most critical part of any cut, so whichever tool and method you use, keep the tool in contact with the wood as long as possible. When roughing with the spindle roughing gouge, cut in both directions and build up the flow and rhythm. When using the deep-fluted gouge and unsupported entry, at the end of a cut slide the tool back along the surface and the tool will return to the start position, ready to make the same cut again. For the scraping cuts, float backwards and forward over the wood surface without losing contact. If the procedure has flow and rhythm, the finished piece will quickly appear.

Making a floating entry

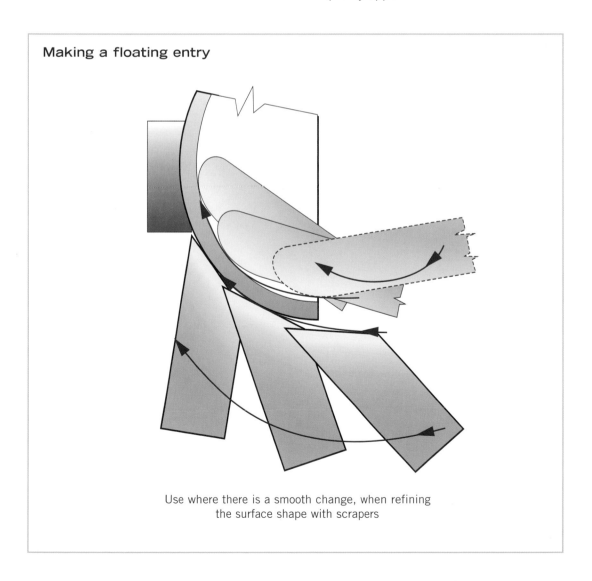

Use where there is a smooth change, when refining the surface shape with scrapers

Controlling the tool

Tool control is really what woodturning is all about; knowing exactly how to manipulate the tool and then control its progress through the wood, so that the desired shape emerges at the end. There are two kinds of tool, each of which is controlled differently: gouges and chisels, which have bevel contact on the wood; and scrapers, which have edge contact on the wood.

Gouges and chisels

Control is achieved through the contact of the bevel on the wood, behind the cutting edge in the direction of cut. There are two elements to control: the **forces** on the tool and the **direction** the bevel is facing.

Forces

By applying a force along the tool handle with the control hand, there are two forces created between the bevel of the tool and the cut wood surface. The first is what I call a **stability** force, which is 90° to the bevel and keeps the bevel on the wood. The second is a **feed** force, which drives the tool through the wood and the force is parallel to the bevel.

A The DFG, with a flat bevel, best illustrates this principle. The bevel is lined up in the direction for making the cut and by pushing along the handle with the control hand, the tool will make a cut following the direction the bevel is facing. In this case, as the bevel angle is 45°, these forces are equal.

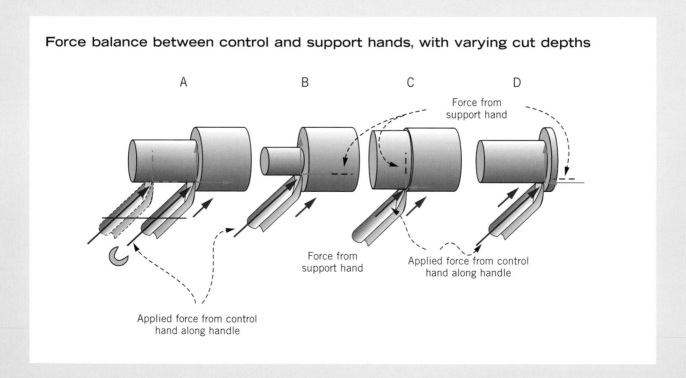

Force balance between control and support hands, with varying cut depths

A   B   C   D

Force from support hand

Force from support hand

Applied force from control hand along handle

Applied force from control hand along handle

Effect of bevel angle on the balance of feed and stability forces

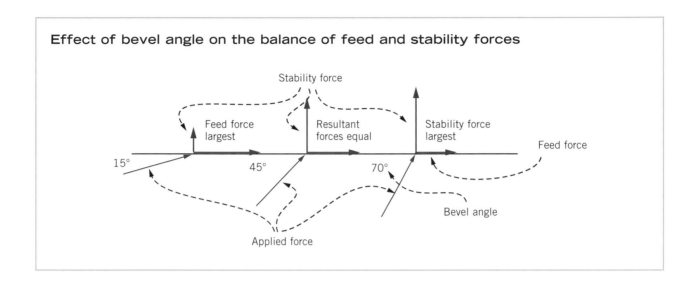

Stability force

Feed force largest

Resultant forces equal

Stability force largest

Feed force

15°

45°

70°

Bevel angle

Applied force

B When making a regular-sized cut, say about ⅛–¼in (3–6mm) deep, the balance of forces is about right and it just needs force down the handle to make the cut. For a larger cut more feed force is needed, but increasing the force down the handle also increases the stability force, putting greater pressure on the wood from the bevel. This pressure can become excessive, causing the soft grain to depress under the bevel, then the hard grain pushes the bevel out again. This starts a vibration that shows up on the surface of the wood. To avoid this for deeper cuts, the extra feed force should be provided by the support hand pushing in the direction of cut.

C Conversely, reducing the feed force for a finer cut in turn reduces the stability force to the point where it is no longer adequate and causes loss of control. Therefore, the support hand should press the bevel onto the wood to maintain the stability.

D To slow down a cut, usually at the end to maintain control, the control hand should continue the push, while the support hand applies pressure in the opposite direction to the feed, thus slowing down the cut. In this way the tool will go through the end of the cut without any breakaway.

The split of the force between feed and stability is dependent on the bevel angle. Using a skew chisel with a 15° bevel, hardly any of the pressure down

the handle is transferred to the stability force, so this is provided by the support hand. When the SRG is presented square to the wood, the control hand only provides the stability force and all the feed force is supplied by the support hand.

The spindle roughing gouge presented square

Square to axis roughing cut

Smoothing cut

Feed force from support hand

Applied force from control hand

Direction When the bevel contact is behind the cutting edge, the tool travels in the direction the bevel is pointing. By moving the end of the handle along at the same speed as the tip, keeping the bevel pointing in a constant direction, then the tool will make a cut in a straight line. If the handle is swung, the direction in which the bevel is pointing will change, thus changing the direction of the cut through the wood.

The diagram illustrates the direction of the DFG. In the first and fifth sections, the tool handle moves at the same speed as the tip, creating a parallel cut. In the second section the handle is slowly swung forward as the cut proceeds, creating a convex curve. In the third section, the handle is swung backwards as the cut proceeds, producing a concave curve.

In the forth section, swinging the handle forward again creates another convex curve.

Swinging the handle, which is a big movement, is fine for creating big curves such as on bowls. When it comes to small details, such as beads and coves, just swinging the handle is a very clumsy movement, so this is where the shallow-fluted gouge with a fingernail grind and the skew chisel both come in. For both of these tools, when the handle is presented square to the wood, the cutting edge is in a sheer presentation and bevel contact is behind the cutting edge. Just twisting the tool handle changes the direction the bevel is pointing and so changes the direction of cut. The amount of curve that can be achieved with just a twist is dependent on the bevel angle (when using the cutting edge of the skew,

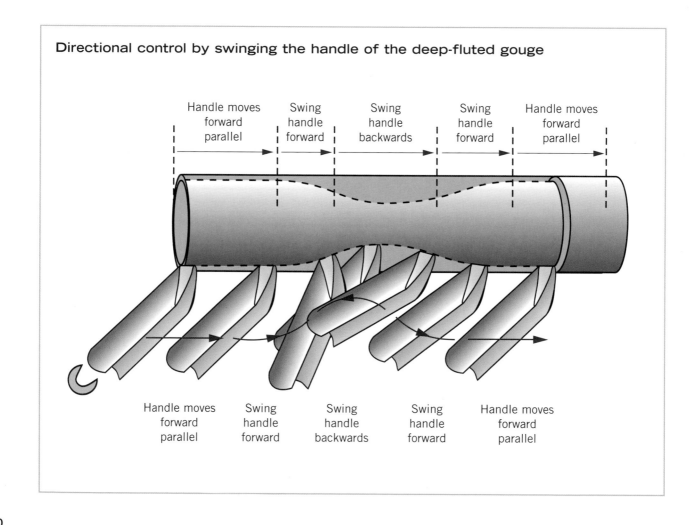

Directional control by swinging the handle of the deep-fluted gouge

Handle moves forward parallel | Swing handle forward | Swing handle backwards | Swing handle forward | Handle moves forward parallel

Handle moves forward parallel | Swing handle forward | Swing handle backwards | Swing handle forward | Handle moves forward parallel

Making curved shapes

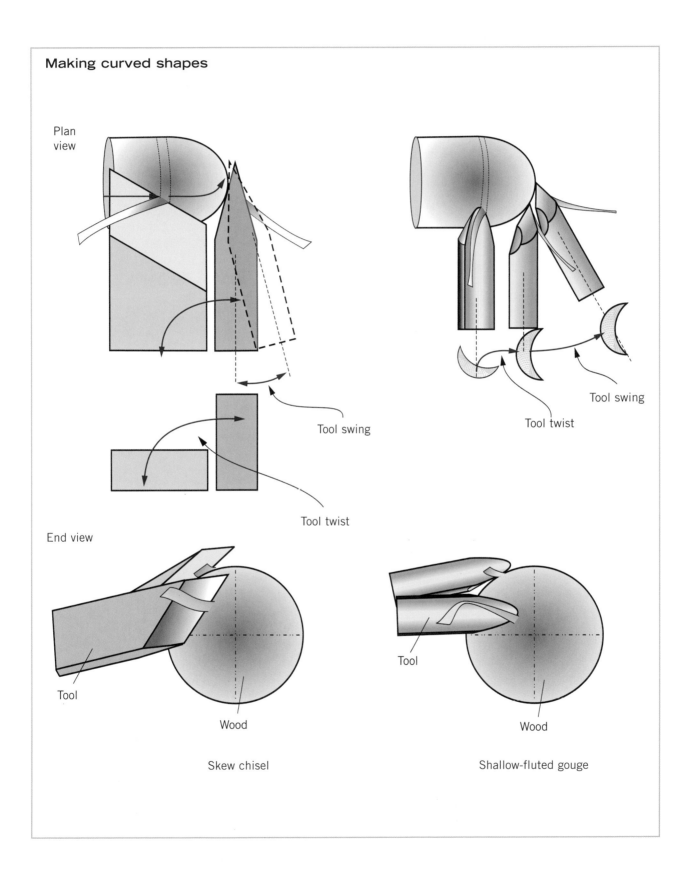

Plan view

Tool swing

Tool twist

Tool swing

Tool twist

End view

Tool

Wood

Skew chisel

Tool

Wood

Shallow-fluted gouge

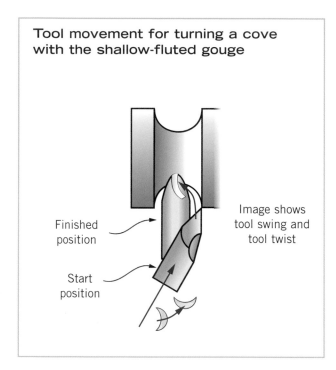

Tool movement for turning a cove with the shallow-fluted gouge

Finished position

Start position

Image shows tool swing and tool twist

the axis. The finish position is with the tool flat on its back at 90° to the axis. To move from the start position the tool is twisted 90° and swung by the bevel angle of 30°. I must admit that I have found coves easier to cut with a 20° bevel angle on a shallow-fluted gouge as there is more control with less swing of the tool.

Scrapers

With scrapers there is no bevel contact, only edge contact on the wood. Therefore there is no control surface as with gouges and chisels. The scraper will go whichever way it is pulled or pushed with either hand. While the control hand takes the weight of the handle and swings it, either hand can provide the feed and movement depending on the cut. Stability is provided by the weight of the tool and the contact of the control hand on the tool rest (as well, of course, as taking a strong dynamic stance).

General shapes Where the cutting edge is relatively square to the tool, then the support hand provides the feed. Where the cutting edge is significantly skewed to the tool axis, then either hand can provide the feed force.

Shape control Shape control is made firstly by choosing a scraper with an edge shape close to the shape to be cut and the larger the tool the better (within reason). A good size would be 1½in (38mm) wide. By swinging the handle while feeding the tool, the shape being cut is controlled. There is quite a bit of 'feel' in the process.

Specific shapes When turning beads or coves with a specially scraped scraper, the shape can be created simply by pushing them into the wood.

not the point). Take a curve, turned with a skew chisel that has a 15° bevel angle and 60° skew angle. With the handle square to the axis and the bevel laid flat on the spindle, slide the tool forward, twisting at the same time to make a cut until the tool is vertical. This will have created a 75° curve. To get the extra 15° the tool should be swung 15° while twisting.

Doing the same cut with the shallow-fluted gouge with a bevel angle of 30° and then twisting will only produce a 60° curve. The handle should be swung 30° to make a 90° curve. Only a tool with a 0° bevel angle will not need any swing, but then the tool becomes handed and not so flexible.

Making a cove with the shallow-fluted gouge is almost the reverse of a convex curve. The tool starts in a direct entry position, with the bevel at 90° to

Working with the grain

When cutting wood, the tool needs to 'flow with the grain' in order to produce clean-cut surfaces. It is a good, general principle from which to start, but there are situations where it is difficult or impossible to cut exactly with the grain. In such circumstances, an understanding of grain flow and cutting direction will help you to achieve a good finish.

Ideally timber should be planked parallel to the grain – the grain flow you would get if you cleaved or split the wood from the log. When the wood is prepared like this, it can be planed in either direction along the grain to produce a smooth, fine finish (**A** and **B**). If the wood is planed across the grain, the result would be a rough finish (**C**).

When the grain isn't parallel to the surface, the cut can still be in flow with the grain, in order to achieve a good finish, but only in one direction (**D**). If you try cutting in the opposite direction it will be against the grain flow, the cut will be difficult to make and it will result in a very rough surface (**E**). Again, cutting across the grain will result in a poor surface (**F**).

On a piece of wood where the grain is wavy and changes direction, there would be smooth areas and areas of very rough surface when making a cut in either direction along the grain. Overall, the surface would be very difficult to deal with. In this situation a cabinet-maker would angle the plane (cutting edge) by up to 45° and make a cut along the grain (**G**). This evens out the quality of the surface; it greatly improves the quality of the rough area, while slightly reducing the quality of the good area.

It is interesting to note that it is just the angle of the cutting edge, relative to the grain direction, that changed – not the direction of movement of the cutting edge. This is important for the woodturner because, similarly, it is the direction in which the cutting edge is facing, relative to the grain direction, and not the direction it is moving (nor the wood rotating), that makes a difference to the quality of the cut surface.

Another situation where the grain isn't parallel to the surface being cut is when cutting a chamfer. Here again, a good quality finish can only be obtained by cutting in one direction (**H**) and cutting in the opposite direction will produce a poor result (**I**).

Effect of cutting with chisel or plane on parallel grain wood

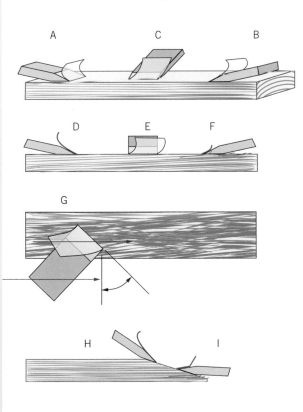

Spindle turning

When the grain of the wood runs parallel to the lathe axis, the cutting edge should face along the grain in order to get the best finish (**A** and **B**). In this position, none of the cutting edge is facing the rotation of the wood and therefore no wood will be removed. With the cutting edge parallel to the lathe axis (**C**), the cutting edge is fully facing the rotation of the wood. In this position, lots of wood will be removed, but as the cutting edge faces across the grain, a rough finish will be produced. Swing the cutting edge round, so it is about 45° to the lathe axis, and make a cut along the spindle to produce a good surface finish.

This is a 45° shear peeling cut. In a situation where the grain isn't parallel to the surface as the wood rotates, one side will be cut with the grain and one against it – this side changes with a change in tool direction. The shear angle can be changed to optimize the finish on the wood.

Where the diameter changes, such as on a chamfer, the tool should face away from the large diameter and towards the small diameter to cut with the grain. If it faces the opposite way, the finish will be rough.

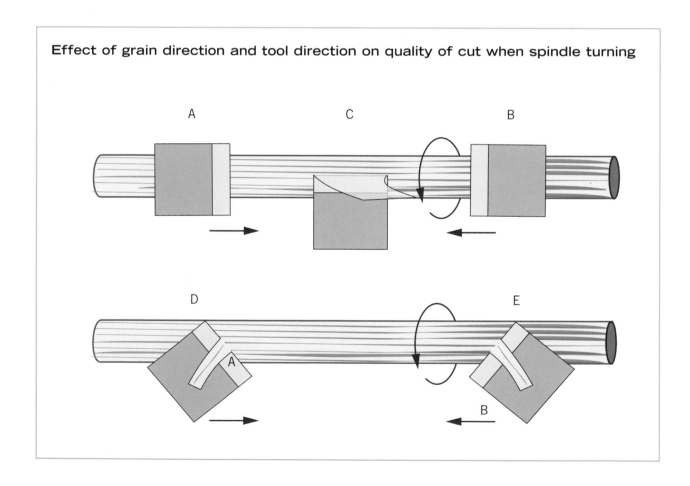

Effect of grain direction and tool direction on quality of cut when spindle turning

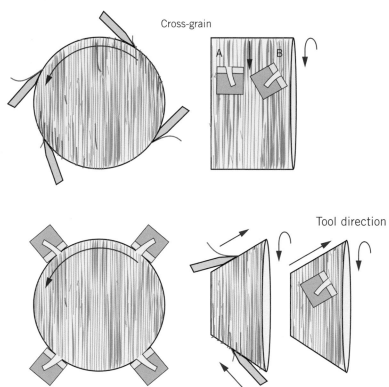

Effect of grain direction and tool direction on quality of cut when turning cross-grain wood

Cross-grain

The wood is turning anti-clockwise

Tool direction

Cutting cross-grain

Cutting cross-grain is completely different to spindle turning. Presenting the tool for a peeling cut will produce different results around the parallel blank as the grain changes – that is, going from cutting directly with the grain to cutting directly against it. Bringing the shear angle to 60° points the tool with the grain, so evening out and improving the overall finish.

By swinging the cutting edge round to a shear peeling cut, the overall quality of the cut greatly improves. But parallel-sided bowls are a rarity. A vee-shape would be a more representative shaped bowl. Again, swinging the cutting edge round to a shear peeling cut will improve the surface, but only if it faces in the direction of the large diameter. Similar improvements in surface finish can also be achieved when scrapers are presented in the shear position – a shear scraping cut. Conversely, on the inside of cross-grain work, the tool should point from the large diameter to the small diameter.

Tip
Remember: the quality of the surface finish is dependent on the direction the tool is facing, not the direction it is moving. The quality of the surface finish for any piece of wood is dependent on how the grain runs through the wood. This can be adjusted by altering the shear angle of the cutting edge.

Chucking the wood

When working on a lathe that can run at speeds of up to 2,500rpm, you must ensure that the wood is held securely in the lathe, with no chance of it coming off. Even at slower speeds a large, out-of-balance piece of wood can become an unpredictable missile in the workshop if the fixing isn't reliable. The holding method should allow access all around the wood, so that the tool can make the cuts, and it should not influence the design of the object. Many pieces, particularly bowls and boxes, need to be held in two or three different ways, but the finished piece should bear no indication of the holding methods used.

Between centres

Mounting between centres is done primarily for spindle turning, where the grain runs parallel to the lathe axis through the length of the piece and is only turned on the outside. The wood is supported at both ends, which allows the turning of long, slender spindles, such as table legs. Items such as goblets, end-grain bowls and hollow vessels can also be mounted between centres.

Find the centre of each end using a gauge or a straightedge and pencil. Mark the centre with a round, fine-pointed bradawl. The bradawl should have a finer point than the drive and tail centres. On soft wood the blank could be placed between the centre points, then the tailstock tightened until the drive dogs penetrate the wood to provide a positive drive. Alternatively, hammer the drive centre onto a blank on the bench to create indents so that the drive centre will positively penetrate the wood without the need for excessive pressure from the tailstock.

Above Using fingers as a gauge to find the centre of a square.

Right Marking the centre with a fine-pointed bradawl.

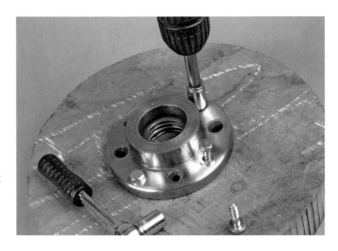

Right Using power driver and ratchet to fit faceplate.

My favourite method for square wood is to cut diagonal lines on the bandsaw. Place one edge in the groove in the table, line up the top edge with the blade and push the wood to cut a shallow groove. Repeat on the next corner. This also finds the centre, which I mark with a fine-pointed bradawl. If you don't have a groove in-line with the blade, take a piece of plywood and cut a straight line halfway along it. Stop the machine, turn the wood round and replace it so that the cut groove is in front of the teeth. Clamp it on the table and you are ready to make positive locations for the drive centre.

At the drive end, use a regular four-pronged centre on larger work where the end of the wood is square. Use a regular two-pronged centre when the end is irregular or not square, to ensure that the prongs penetrate evenly. On small work, use a small, four-pronged drive centre or a steb centre (up to 1in or 25mm diameter). At the tailstock end, use a regular revolving cone centre for hardwoods and a regular revolving cup centre for softwoods.

Long-hole boring This method describes how to mount centres for long-hole boring. At the tailstock end, use a cup centre with a removable point for both hardwoods and softwoods. When the blank has been roughed down, remove the point in the cup centre and bore the hole. Replace the drive centre with a counter bore and replace the point in the cup centre. Reverse the piece and locate the hole on the pin of the counterbore. Tighten up the tailstock so that the rim of the cup makes a positive, locating mark on the wood. Remove the point from the cup centre, then remount the wood, locating the cup in the groove created. Bore through the hollow tailstock.

Faceplate

The surface of the blank should be flat. Use at least four screws – strong ones, such as Philips-head screws that will penetrate more than ½in (13mm) depending on the size of the blank. Mark the hole centres with a bradawl, then use a power screwdriver to fix the screws in place. On pieces over 12in (305mm) in diameter, use coach screws with a hexagonal head for an extra firm grip.

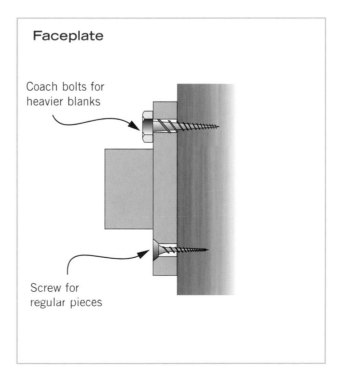

Faceplate

Coach bolts for heavier blanks

Screw for regular pieces

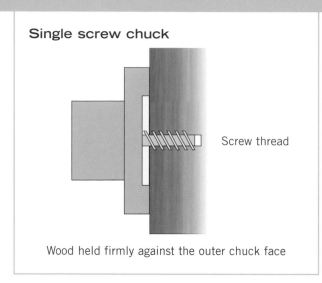

Screw thread

Wood held firmly against the outer chuck face

Single screw

Make sure the surface on which to fit on the chuck is reasonably flat. Drill a hole the same diameter as the pin diameter of the screw and a little deeper than the length of the pin. Lock the lathe spindle and screw the blank firmly onto the screw chuck.

Contracting jaws

Contracting jaws hold onto a spigot. They need to have contact on a flat surface to give the piece stability. This could be on the face of the spigot, if the spigot is longer than the jaws **(A)**, or on the step of the spigot if this is shorter than the jaws **(B)**. The shape of the dovetails is important: ideally they should match the jaws or be less dovetailed. If the shape is more dovetailed, the initial grip will only be on the edge of the dovetail, which can crush easily, causing the blank to move in the chuck and run out of true, possibly weakening the grip.

Preparation

Clean the face of the blank and mark the diameter of the spigot with a pencil. Use a deep-fluted gouge to make a cut down to about ¼in (6mm) above the diameter of the spigot **(C)**. Line up the bevel, either parallel or slightly dovetailed (but not more dovetailed than the jaws). Make two cuts for the spigot. Make a light cut to clean the back face if the spigot is shorter than the jaws. Alternatively, shape a scraper to the dovetail angle with two cutting faces **(D)**.

Jaws contracting on a spigot

A   B

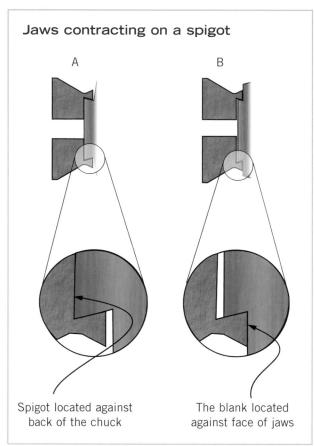

Spigot located against back of the chuck

The blank located against face of jaws

Turning a spigot with different gouges

C   D

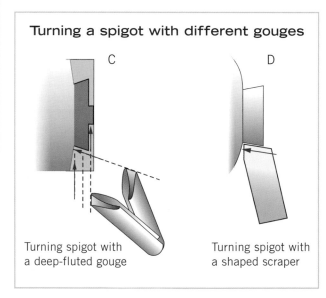

Turning spigot with a deep-fluted gouge

Turning spigot with a shaped scraper

Square and round section held in centre section of jaws

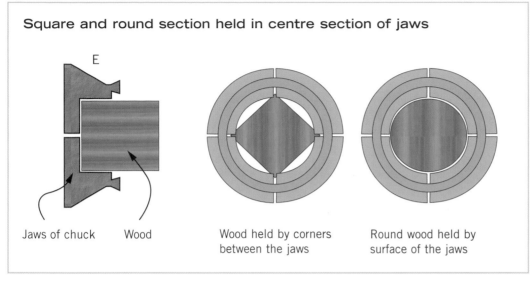

E

Jaws of chuck   Wood

Wood held by corners
between the jaws

Round wood held by
surface of the jaws

Below Fitting
spigot in to
contracting jaws.

Fitting

Open the jaws so that the spigot fits in easily and in
contact with the face. Keep pressing in the centre
with the right hand while the left hand tightens the
jaws. Use both hands to make the final tightening.

Short sections of square or round can be held
directly in the jaws with a long recess inside and do
not need any preparation – ideal for egg cups, door
knobs and so on **(E)**.

Expanding chuck

Use the expanding chuck on items with a large base,
such as platters and trays, where plenty of wood can
be left around the recess for strength and this does
not dictate the size of the base.

Left Recess for expanding chuck.

Detail of expanding jaws located against back of recess

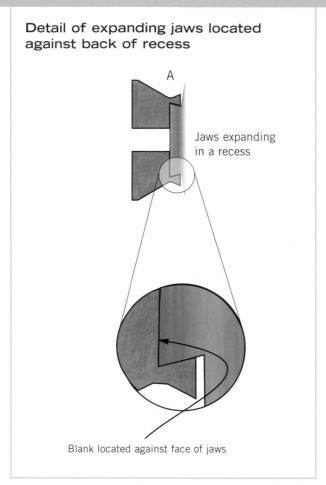

A

Jaws expanding in a recess

Blank located against face of jaws

Turning recess for expanding jaws with shaped scraper

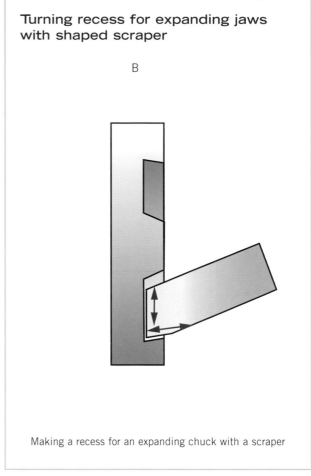

B

Making a recess for an expanding chuck with a scraper

Preparation

When the base is otherwise finished, mark the outside diameter and the inner diameter of the jaws – you will only be removing the area between these two measurements. Again, contact is needed on a flat area, to give stability to the piece. In this case it is the face of the jaws on the bottom of the recess **(A)**.

Removing just the groove is best done with a specially shaped scraper, which has a flat surface on the end and a dovetail on the left-hand side **(B)**. This should be slightly less dovetailed than the jaws so that the grip is in the bottom of the recess. Make light cuts to take the groove down from ⅛in (3mm) to ¼in (6mm) deep, depending on the size of the piece, then undercut the dovetail.

As this is likely to be the finished base, soften the corner of the dovetail and make some decoration in the centre section. Sand and finish so it is ready for mounting.

Mounting

Use both hands to position the piece over the jaws. Use one hand to hold the piece in position while the other hand tightens the jaws. Tighten enough to be secure but don't over tighten as this may result in bursting the supporting wood.

Pin chuck

I use a pin chuck for natural-edged bowls where there is no flat face for mounting, or for large, flat-topped bowls as an alternative to a faceplate.

Preparation

Use a sawtooth or Forstner bit for an accurate hole and check the drill is sharp. Set the depth stop to go in far enough for the secondary pin to be against solid wood. At a slow speed, drill the hole in one pass for a clean, accurate hole.

Mounting
Lock the lathe spindle with the flat of the pin chuck
facing up and horizontal. Place the secondary pin
in the centre. Push the blank over the pins without
twisting. When fully located, rotate the blank in the
opposite direction to lathe rotation, until the blank is
firmly locked on the chuck.

To remove the piece, lock the spindle again and
rotate the piece in the direction of lathe rotation until
it is loose, then slide it off.

Jam chuck

Jam chucks are used for holding a bowl on the
inside (or outside) of the rim to enable the base to
be turned and finished. This has to be accurate and
made to suit each bowl. Turn a spigot with a slight
leading taper. Hold the rim of the bowl on the taper;
if it goes on almost to the straight section, then a
light tap should push the rim on the spigot. If it is
slightly slack, then put a piece of paper or cloth over
the spigot to make the fit secure.

Cup chuck

The work piece is held on a tapered surface. The
chuck doesn't have to be accurate, as it will accept a
small range of sizes. I use this type of chuck to hold
solid apples. The piece is pressed into the chuck,
with the palm of the hand, and the 'give' of the
chuck creates extra grip. A knock-out bar is usually
necessary to remove the piece (make sure there is a
hole in the chuck).

Waste blocks

These are glued to the blank and used for chucking
to avoid wasting good wood. The bowl blank is held
on the top with a faceplate, the bowl is roughly
shaped and a flat area is made on the bottom.
Whichever glue you use, allow time for it to 'cure'.
If a strong glue is used it might be advisable to put
a piece of brown paper between the glued surfaces
so that they are easier to separate. The waste block
can be turned and a very shallow recess made, which
would locate the faceplate centrally so that the
piece runs fairly true when the piece is remounted.
Alternatively, a spigot could be turned on the waste
block and the piece held in contracting dovetail jaws
– again, to save precious wood. When the turning is
finished, the glue block is parted off.

Locking blank on pin chuck
Rotate wood in opposite direction to lathe rotation to lock on the pin

Rotate in the same direction to lathe rotation to unlock

Right Jam chuck: holding a bowl by the rim on a spigot. Cup chuck: an apple pressed into the chuck for its base to be turned.

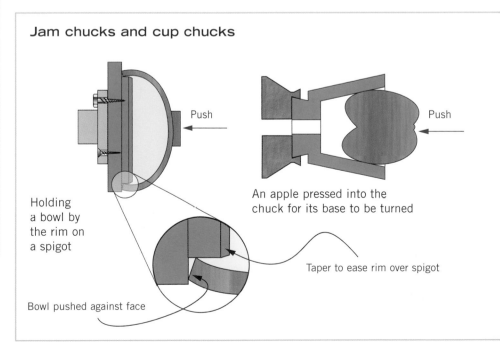

Jam chucks and cup chucks

Push

Holding a bowl by the rim on a spigot

Bowl pushed against face

An apple pressed into the chuck for its base to be turned

Push

Taper to ease rim over spigot

Sharpening the tools

Once your tool sharpening system is close to the lathe, set at a comfortable working height, fitted with suitable wheels and tool rest, you should be ready to sharpen your tools.

Dressing the wheel

The first action is to check the surface of the wheel and dress it as necessary – this should be done on a regular basis to keep the wheel clean, sharp and in shape. I dress my high-speed wheels every day.

High-speed grinders

Whether you use a devil stone, Huntington wheel, diamond cluster or single point diamond, the process is the same: slide the dresser backwards and forward across the wheel surface until it is clean and flat. Ensure you wear eye and breathing protection.

Wetstone grinders

Slow running wide wheels should be dressed with a large surface dresser – by far the quickest method. The Tormek stone grader will do the job, or you could use a devil stone. Hold the dresser level to the wheel axis and apply even pressure while slowly moving it from side to side.

Tip
It isn't necessary to dress a belt grinder – simply change the belt.

Top left Dressing a high-speed wheel with a single diamond in a guide.

Left Grading the Tormek wetstone grinder.

Stance

The length of turning tools means that the best position for sharpening them is at the side of the wheel. Here you are close to the action, in the best position to control the tool movement and to see the sharpening process. It is also the safest as you are out of line of the sparks and anything else that flies off the wheel. Stand to the left of the wheel if you are right-handed, to the right if you are left-handed. If you are using a high-speed grinder you should put the sharpening wheel (the fine one, that you will be using most often) to the same side that you stand. This is so that you do not stretch across the grinder, with the risk of your arm touching the other wheel.

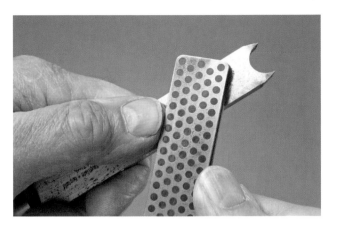

Above Sharpening form tool with a diamond file.

Procedure

Sharpening creates a burr on the cutting edge – the finer the edge angle, the bigger the burr. Where the tool relies on the burr to cut the wood, such as on some scrapers, the old burr should be removed with a diamond file or similar tool before re-sharpening.

If the burr is not required then it can be removed after sharpening, although for most tools, the first cut on the wood will remove the burr. The following process applies to the use of an adjustable platform. If using special jigs follow the manufacturer's instructions. The jig should be set to give the desired

Below Using a jig to sharpen the swept-back grind of a DFG on the Sorby belt grinder.

Above Setting the platform angle on the Sorby belt grinder using the pre-set positions.

shape – never change these settings to achieve repeatability. Set the platform to the bevel angle for the particular tool. Hold the stock of the tool on the rest with straight fingers of the support hand (fingers grip). Hold the handle at the narrowest point with the fingers of the control hand (flexi grip) so that it can be rolled in the fingers. While sharpening is described in individual tool movements, these should flow from one movement to another in continuous action.

Above Setting the platform angle using pre-set positions on the O'Donnell jig for high speed grinders.

Below left Setting the platform on the Tormek grinder using their gauge.

Below Fingers holding the tool on the rest.

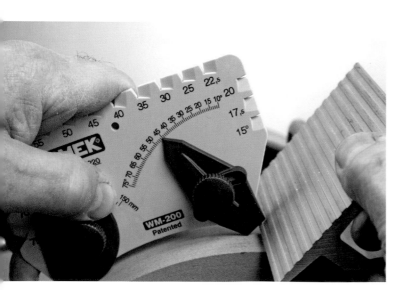

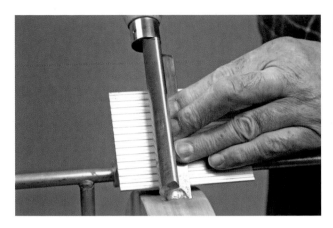

Above Sharpening the SRG on the Tormek platform in the start position; wheel running towards the tool.

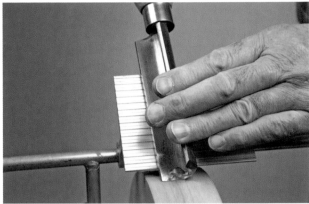

Above Sharpening the SRG on the Tormek platform in the end position; wheel running towards the tool.

Spindle roughing gouge with 45° bevel angle

Place the wing of the spindle roughing gouge flat on the rest, with the flute facing you. Hold the flute on the rest with support hand in fingers grip. Line up the edge with the wheel then push the bevel up against the rotating wheel. Slide the tool backwards and forward across the wheel. Roll the gouge onto the other wing and repeat the sliding (the fingers of the control hand rise up as the flute is rotated). Repeat the sequence as necessary until the whole cutting edge has been ground.

Parting tool/sizing tool with 30/45° bevel angle

Place the tool vertically flat on the tool rest so it is square to the face of the wheel. Hold on the rest with the support hand in fingers grip. Push the bevel up against the rotating wheel. Slide it backwards and forward across the wheel until the cutting edge has been ground. For the sizing tool, sharpen it on one bevel only, then next time make sure you sharpen it on the second bevel.

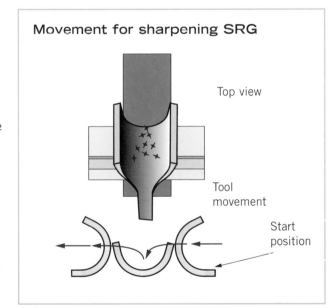

Movement for sharpening SRG

Top view

Tool movement

Start position

Right Sharpening parting tool on lower bevel.

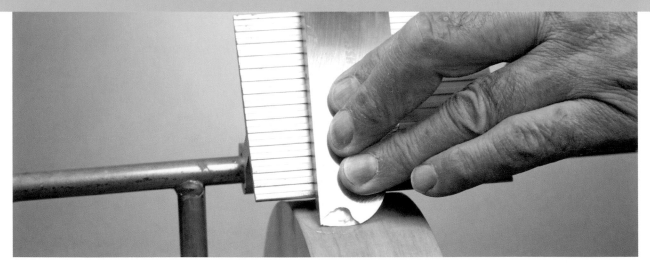

Above Swinging scraper on Tormek wetstone.

Scraper with 45° bevel angle

Place the scraper flat on the rest and hold on with the support hand in fingers grip.

For **straight-edged scrapers**, line up the edge with the face of the wheel. Push the tool onto the wheel. Slide it backwards and forward across the wheel until the cutting edge has been ground.

For **curved-edge scrapers**, push the tool onto the wheel. Swing the handle backwards and forward to grind the whole of the cutting edge.

Above A skew chisel using a guide located in the platform.

Skew chisel with 15° bevel angle

Place the chisel flat on the rest and hold on with the control hand in fingers grip (use a skew guide if available).

For **straight-edged chisels**, line up the edge with the face of the wheel. Use a guide if available. Push the tool onto the wheel. Slide it backwards and forward across the wheel until the cutting edge has been ground.

For **curved-edge chisels**, hold the chisel on the rest with the thumb of the control hand and the fingers gripping under the platform. Keep fingers away from the wheel. Push the tool onto the wheel to touch in the centre of the cutting edge. Swing the handle backwards and forward to grind the whole of the cutting edge. Only sharpen one bevel; next time sharpen on the other bevel.

Left Curved skew held with thumb.

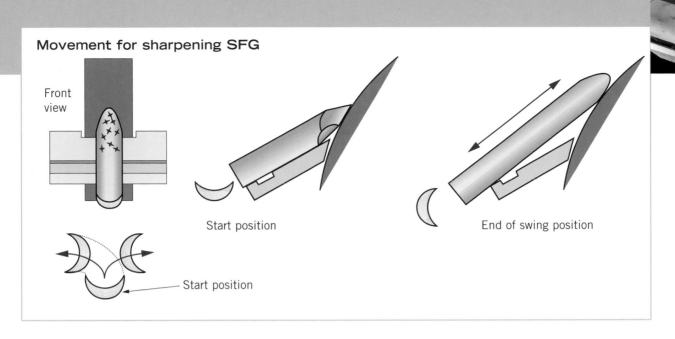

Movement for sharpening SFG

Front view

Start position

End of swing position

Start position

Shallow-fluted gouge with 30° bevel angle

1 Place the chisel flat on the rest and hold on with the control hand in fingers grip. Push the bevel against the wheel.

2 Rotate the tool just under 90° towards you and at the same time push it up the wheel about ¾in (19mm), keeping the stock on the back edge of the platform. Reverse the movement back onto the platform. Repeat step 2, bringing the tool back on to the platform.

3 Rotate the tool just under 90° away from you and at the same time push it up the wheel about ¾in (19mm) keeping the stock on the back edge of the platform. Reverse the movement back onto the platform. Repeat step 3.

4 With the gouge flat on the rest, roll the tool to create the round end.

Deep-fluted gouge with 45° bevel angle

1 Place the gouge flat on the rest and hold on with the control hand with a fingers grip. Push the bevel against the wheel.

2 Rotate the tool just under 180° towards you and at the same time push it up the wheel about 1¼in (32mm), keeping the stock on the back edge of the platform. Reverse the movement back onto the platform. Repeat step 2.

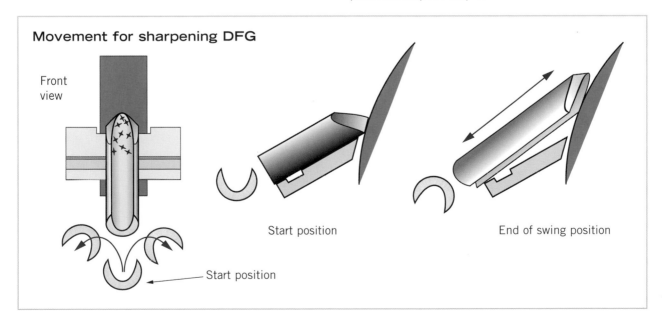

Movement for sharpening DFG

Front view

Start position

End of swing position

Start position

3 Rotate the tool just under 180° away from you and at the same time push it up the wheel about 1¼in (32mm), keeping the stock on the back edge of the platform. Reverse the movement back onto the platform. Repeat step 3.

4 Roll the tool on the rest to create the round end.

Secondary bevel
To put a secondary bevel on gouges, set the platform to give a secondary bevel angle about 15° higher than the primary bevel angle. Place the gouge on the rest and make contact on the wheel. Roll the gouge backwards and forward to create the bevel, being careful not to grind the edge.

Form tools
Form tools are sharpened on the top surface with a slip stone or diamond file. This can be done at a slight angle, creating a negative rake, so as to minimize the area of sharpening.

Above Manoeuvring the DFG in start position to achieve the swept-back grind.

Above Manoeuvring the DFG in mid-position to achieve the swept-back grind.

Right Sharpening form tool with diamond file.

Long-hole boring

When I attended my first woodturning class back in 1972, the guy on the next lathe to me was making a standard lamp, about 4ft tall, which required a hole down the centre for the wire. The instructor's method of making the hole was to saw the blank down the middle, carve a groove down the centre of the two halves, then glue them back together. Certainly it worked and I am sure the lamp is still in use, but there are other ways to put the hole down the centre that are quicker and do not need glue.

The principle of long-hole boring is to pass a long drill or auger through a hollow tailstock that both supports the wood and acts as a guide for the auger. An auger is a long, fluted round bar with a cutting lip at the tip; this lip also serves to pull out the shavings as the auger is removed.

Using a standard auger to bore from both ends

1 Use a four-prong drive in the headstock and a revolving cup centre with a removable pin in the tailstock. The diameter of the pin should be the same as the auger so that the auger is automatically guided to the centre.

2 Only rough down the blank to round before boring the hole. Sometimes the augers do not go straight, which means the nicely finished work on the outside could be wasted.

3 Remount the wood with the pin removed from the tailstock. Reduce the lathe speed to about 200–300rpm.

Below Auger in hollow cup centre.

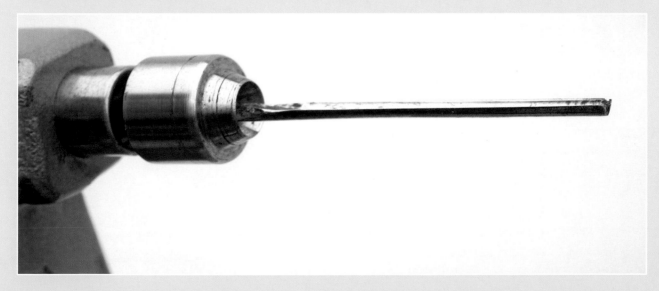

Right Feeding the auger through the tailstock into the wood.

4 Lay the auger on the wood in the lathe, with the tip at the maximum depth of the hole. Put a chalk mark on the auger at the end of the tailstock so that you know when to stop.

5 Use the auger with the flute facing upwards to carry the wood-shavings out of the hole. If the shavings fall off inside the tailstock, then this can become blocked and prevent the auger from re-entering the wood.

6 Hold the auger in line with the lathe axis, then firmly push it into the wood by about 1in (25mm). Remove and clear the wood-shavings. Repeat the process in 1in (25mm) stages until the hole is beyond the halfway mark in the wood. Remove the wood, change the drive to a counter bore and replace the point in the tailstock. Tighten up the tailstock until the cup ring makes a positive location in the wood. Remove the pin from the tailstock, remount the wood and proceed to bore – with any luck the holes will meet in the middle.

7 Replace the point in the tailstock so that it extends into the hole and provides a very secure holding. The outside can then be turned and finished.

Boring from one end

If the length of the wood plus tailstock is shorter than the drill, then it can be bored right through in one operation. Either hold the wood in a chuck at the drive end, which will allow the auger to go right through the wood, or leave on extra waste wood, which can be cut off where the drilled hole stops. When the piece is to be a table lamp or similar, where the base is larger in diameter then the top, I always bore from the base end first to ensure that I can get the maximum diameter, even if the auger runs off slightly.

Sanding

Sandpaper (a coated abrasive) is the last cutting tool that you use on wood. Always make sure that the dust extractor is switched on and that you wear a face mask. Leave the lathe running at the same speed as used for the turning. Move the tool rest away from the wood, but it can still be used for resting an arm on. Keep the abrasive moving backwards and forwards along the surface to avoid making deep scratches with the grit.

Refining large shapes

The abrasive backing should be firm, so that it just contacts the 'high' spots on the wood and brings them down to smooth. Folding the abrasive twice to make three thicknesses gives added strength, but it is much better to wrap the abrasive round some padding that is moulded to the shape of the wood. This padding could be anything from a few wood-shavings to a piece of hard foam or wood.

On long, straight spindle work surfaces, use a strong-backed abrasive, about 2–4in (50–100mm) wide. Stretch it over the wood with both hands and keep it moving up and down. This will quickly produce a flat even surface. Wrapping the course grits around a suitably sized dowel will quickly refine the shape of a cove.

Right Abrasive wrapped around wood-shavings to refine the outside shape of the bowl.

Below Using a wide, heavy-backed abrasive to refine the stem of the lamp.

Above Using the cut edge of the abrasive to sand a bead detail.

Above Fingers moulding the abrasive around the wood surface.

On the finer grades, use the fingertips to press the abrasive onto the wood. Follow the surface shape and get into every part of the surface, removing earlier sanding marks. Where there is an edge, such as the rim of a bowl, always work up to the edge to keep it sharp. If you get it too sharp, then a light touch with a fine grit at the end will take the edge off.

Tip
Don't jump intermediate grades as it will take far longer to remove the previous grades marks.

Detail work

For detail work a lighter application is needed; take care not to soften the detail. Use a backing that is flexible enough to follow the shape and get into corners. Then use a 'cut' edge of the abrasive to get into corners.

Sand beads separately on each side, taking the abrasive edge down into the corner, then blend over the top. For sanding a vee, keep the abrasive flat and take the cut edge down into the corner. On delicate stems use the fingers to support the wood.

Above The edge of the abrasive being worked around the detail.

Left Fingers supporting the slim stem.

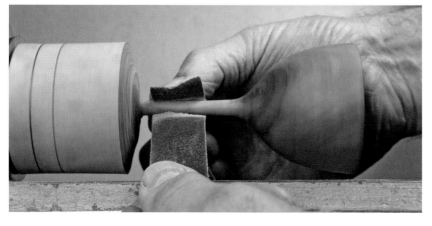

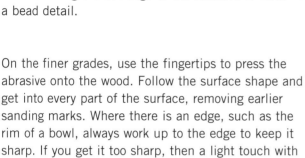

112

Above Power sanding the inside of a bowl.

Right Power sanding the outside of a bowl.

Grits

Start with 80 grit on a piece such as a wet-green turned bowl, work up through 120 and 180 and finish with 240. A 150/180 grit, or even 240, would be suitable for starting on a delicate box or lace bobbin, finishing with a 400/600 grit.

Power sanding

Power sanding is a great way of using abrasives quickly to clean up bowls and large vessels that have long, simple curved surfaces. For concave surfaces, such as inside a bowl, place the tool rest well away from the wood so that the forearm of your support hand can rest comfortably on it. Hold the trigger handle in the control hand. Hold the nose/chuck of the drill with your support hand – this forms the fulcrum around which the drill will pivot so that the sanding disk will flow over the wood surface.

Take a dynamic stance, switch on the lathe and bring the disc into contact with the wood. Ensure that the lead edge of the disc does not touch the wood as this would make an aggressive cut and the disk is more likely to be pushed off the pad. It does not matter whether you work on the upside or the downside of the wood – it will depend on which hand you use to hold the drill. Always keep the disc moving over the surface and work very carefully up to the edges.

For sanding convex surfaces, such as the outside of a bowl, the stance and support are different. Take a dynamic stance and hold the drill in the hands as for a concave surface, but keep the elbows against the body for stability. While working on the regular side of the lathe, hold the drill in the left hand to give access around the base of the bowl near the headstock. Swing the whole of the body in order to flow the disc over the whole surface of the bowl.

Tip

Use a size and hardness of pad that will easily mould to the surface shape. Take care near the centre as it is very easy to dig a hole. Also take care near the rims, working up to them to keep the detail. Sometimes I use a 3in (76mm) pad on a 2in (51mm) disc as this gets round the tighter curves.

Sanding aids

Sanding aids make it easier and quicker to sand the surface and any troublesome areas. They can also help achieve a better surface and can be used as a base for the final finish. The choice of sanding aid depends on its compatibility with the final finish to be used.

Sanding sealer

A sanding sealer is a varnish that contains about 20% fine solid particles, traditionally wood dust, to fill and seal the open pores of the wood and create a smooth surface. It also hardens any loose or torn grains and makes them easier to remove with sanding. The sealed surface is a base for the final finish.

Sand the whole of the piece with 180/240 grit abrasive. Then rotate the wood by hand (or run at 15–25rpm) and use a brush to apply the sanding sealer quickly and thinly – any excess will cause runs. Allow some natural drying time so that the sealer penetrates the grain. Friction dry, at a slow lathe speed (50rpm) so that the sealer isn't spun to the surface and use a soft cloth, keeping it moving over the wood surface; change the cloth as it becomes dirty. Once dry, the lathe speed can be increased for further sanding. Sand again with 240 grit, then finish with finer grits if required.

For particularly troublesome grain, make a local application of sealer at an earlier sanding stage. It can also be reapplied as finer grits are used, but be sure to allow the sealer to dry sufficiently, otherwise it will quickly clog the abrasive.

Other finishes

There are other finishes and wetting agents that can be used as sanding aids, such as wax, polish, lacquer, varnish and water. These can be applied either locally or to the whole piece.

There is no need to allow oils to dry before sanding; indeed, it is good to use them wet as they provide lubrication and a cooling effect. However, the heat generated by the friction of sanding will accelerate drying, so keep the surface wet by dipping the abrasive in the oil. Use a special container for this to avoid getting grit in the oil used for the finish. Wipe off any sludge with a clean cloth and clean the surface with a damp cloth.

Water is a good sanding aid as it can be used whatever the final finish – once it is dry, it leaves no residue. Use water locally on difficult grain, at any stage of sanding. Raising the grain should not be a problem. If the wood is turned green and kept wet during the process, a bucket of water is good for washing the sanding sludge from the abrasive and keeping it clean.

Cleaning

When sanding is finished, the grain will probably be full of dust. To clean this out, either use a light brush or wipe the surface using a cloth dampened with a solvent or water. The surface of the wood is now ready for its final finish.

Olive oil is suitable for contact with food.

Applying finishes

This is the last stage in making your piece and it can be dramatic: the application of a finish instantly brings out the natural colour and figure in the wood and also adds a tactile quality to the piece.

Choosing finishes

Choosing the appropriate finish for a piece will depend largely on personal preference; however, you should also take into account how the finish will be maintained, its suitability for the purpose and its compatibility between coats.

Maintenance

A piece might look really good when you take it off the lathe but this is only the start of its life. Once it has been in a household for a time then some aftercare will be necessary. It might just be a light dusting with a soft cloth, the application of a wax polish, or a wipe with a suitable oil. Whatever it is, it should be as easy as possible and not require the purchase of any special materials. That way there is a good chance it will be lovingly cared for.

Items that come into regular, intimate contact with food – such as rolling pins, breadboards and wooden spoons – don't really require a finish. There is no risk of contaminating food and washing or immersing in water would probably remove most of the finish anyway. However, if selling a piece through a craft shop, where it is likely to be handled by customers, then a light finish is essential to avoid dirty finger marks. A light, 'food-safe' finish will provide suitable protection (see below). Once in the kitchen a wash in warm water is all the maintenance they will need, although there would be no harm in applying a little oil occasionally.

At the other end of the scale, for pieces that are purely decorative (or artistic), a simple dusting will bring them back to life. Adding anything else could change the nature and colour of the surface and detract from the intention of the artist. A hard finish, which totally seals and fills the surface, is probably the easiest to care for. It doesn't have to be high gloss – the nature of the surface will depend on the product used and the final treatment of the surface. I mainly use Craftlac Melamine.

In between these extremes almost anything goes; even allowing some pieces to build up a patina

Above Applying a finish with a brush on a slow-running lathe.

Above right Friction drying and polishing the finish.

Above Brushing a finish onto spindle work.

through handling. You only need to watch an antiques programme to see how the experts set store by acquired patina.

Suitability

For items such as salad or fruit bowls, only use a finish that is described as 'food safe' on the tin. The same applies to toys – look for products that are described as 'toy safe' and for all products, read the small print on the tins. It is likely that the product will only be food or toy safe after about 30 days, once all the volatile organic compounds (VOCs) have evaporated.

These days lead and mercury are no longer used in products and there is an argument that all finishes are therefore food and toy safe – once all the VOCs have evaporated. This may well be true, but it is still advisable to only use finishes that are marked as toy or food safe.

Compatibility

There can be compatibility problems when applying different finishes, causing adverse reactions. If you are using a stain first, make sure that the next finish coat is of a different base to avoid reactivating and changing the stain. Make sure the surface is dry before applying another coat of the same finish; again, reactivation can be a problem and becomes exacerbated by aggressive applications.

Avoid applying a paste wax with wire wool on top of a cellulose finish, as the wire wool will cause excessive mixing and, with the turpentine, may remove all of the cellulose. Oils are best applied to bare wood so that they penetrate and become part of the wood. Waxes can be applied on top of any other finish as well as on bare wood.

Methods of application

Most finishes, except hard waxes, are best applied to wood that is either revolved by hand or in a very slow-running lathe, allowing the finish to penetrate the wood. At times like this I really love my variable speed Vicmarc lathe because I can slow the speed right down to about 20rpm, leaving both hands free to apply the finish.

Lacquers and oils

Lacquers and oils can be applied with a brush or cloth, but I would use a brush for the very quick-drying lacquers, which seem to dry too quickly on the cloth and leave a streaky surface on the wood. A toothbrush is good to get into any intricate details. Once applied, remove any excess with a cloth to leave a clean, smooth surface, then allow to dry. One of the major requirements for woodturners is an instant finish and this often conflicts with the

drying instructions on the tin from five minutes for some lacquers, up to 12 hours for oils. Even then, while a surface may be dry, it probably isn't hard (cured), which could take anything from overnight to one week. This means that care should be taken with subsequent applications so as not to damage the finish. The drying time can be greatly reduced by generating heat through 'friction drying' with a cloth. Apply light pressure at first and gradually increase the speed of the lathe to turning speed. Keep the cloth moving across the surface to avoid over-heating and damaging local areas.

Once dry, a second coat can be applied and the process repeated. If there is a need to abrade between coats, do it carefully with a very fine, worn abrasive. Wire wool is good but make sure to clean the surface afterwards to remove any broken fragments. Three coats should be enough to give an even finish. After the final coat leave at least overnight for final polishing.

Sprays

Only make spray applications in a well-ventilated environment. Apply three coats, then allow the finish to dry and harden before buffing the surface.

Paste wax

Apply paste wax with a cloth on hand-rotated wood. Allow a few minutes for the wax to harden, then polish on the surface at a low speed. Build up with two or three layers and repeat the process. Once the surface is dry, bring the wood up to turning speed and lightly burnish.

Wire wool could be used to apply wax over a lacquered surface, which would refine the lacquered surface at the same time. Use a very fine wire wool and only light pressure.

Above right Friction application of carnauba wax.

Right Polishing the wax on a spindle.

> **Tip**
> If the paste wax has gone hard in the tin, add a little turpentine to soften it.

Hard wax

Use the lathe at turning speed (or slower, as long as the wax melts). Hold the solid wax against the wood, keeping it moving across the surface so that the wax melts and transfers to the wood. When there is a reasonable coating, use a clean cloth to further melt and spread the wax to an even coverage and burnish the surface. Apply two or three coats to build up the thickness as necessary.

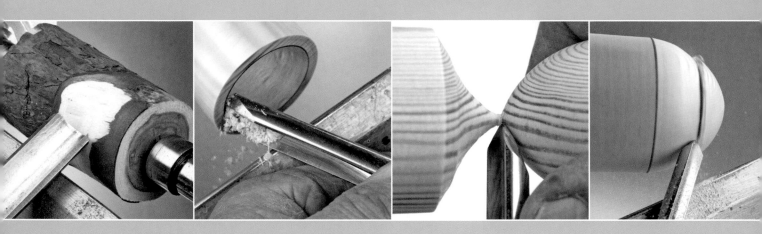

Part three – Turning

With the understanding of the tools, equipment and wood firmly established, we can now bring them all together and start turning. Repetition is the best form of practice. The more you make of one thing, the better you will become. Be methodical in your approach, think about each move. Remember, there are three stages to each cut: the entry, the shaping and the exit. This will bring a pattern and rhythm to your work and make it most enjoyable. What we are looking for is achievement and pleasure.

Spindle roughing gouge

The spindle roughing gouge (SRG) is often the first tool to be used on a spindle (parallel grain) project. It quickly roughs down square to round and leaves a very good surface finish. I find 1¼in 32mm)(a good general size and an 18in (457mm) long handle can do some heavy work. The SRG should not be used on cross-grain work.

Turning

The SRG is used for two basic cuts: for roughing to round and for a finishing cut over a long section.

Set the lathe speed to 1,800rpm. Mount a piece of softwood, 2½in (63mm) square – equivalent to 3½in (89mm) diameter – and 10in (254mm) long, between centres. Set the top of the tool rest ³⁄₁₆in (4mm) below centre height and ½in (12mm) away from the corners of the wood.

Top SRG with long handle.

**Spindle roughing gouge: characteristics
1¼in (32mm) SRG with 18in (457mm) handle**

High-speed steel

Deep forged section with a tang that goes into the handle

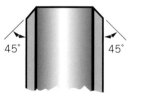

45°   45°

Sharpened square across (front view)

A 45° bevel angle for a strong edge

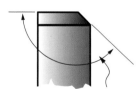

A 135° profile angle for a long edge

Roughing down square stock to round.

Roughing down branches, even with bark.

Roughing down branches, even with bark.

SRG presented for a finishing cut, working from tailstock.

Bevel contact behind cutting edge, working from headstock. Leaves the perfect finish.

Making simple curve shapes, leaving a good finish.

Roughing left-handed; power grip for control hand, fingers grip for support hand.

Right-handed smoothing cut, arm over headstock. Power grip for control hand, fingers grip for support hand.

Roughing cut

For this cut use a large SRG – 1–1¼in (25–31mm). You will be making a supported entry into the wood.

1 Place the tool on the rest at the headstock end, square to the lathe axis, flute up.

2 Stand behind the tool (headstock side) in a dynamic stance, right foot forward, left foot at 90° behind the headstock.

3 Hold the handle of the tool with the right hand in a power grip.

4 Hold the stock in the fingers grip (not touching the tool rest).

5 To check you are comfortable to make the whole cut, slide the tool along the rest backwards and forwards as if making the cut. Depending on the lathe you have, you may find it more comfortable to bring your left arm on top of the headstock. There are some advantages to being left-handed as I stand at the tailstock end for this cut, with the tool in the opposite hand.

6 Without moving your feet, move the tool away from the rest and switch on the lathe.

7 Now place the tool on the middle of the rest, with the cutting edge above the wood. Bring the bevel (or back of the tool) down into contact with the wood, then slide the tool down the wood slowly until tiny wood shavings just appear and hold the tool in that position.

8 The SRG should be in the peeling position with the bevel contact under the cutting edge. With both hands, slide the tool along the rest, holding the bevel against the wood and make the first cut.

9 At the end of the cut, just slide the tool back along the wood, cutting in the opposite direction without removing the tool from the wood. Keep going backwards and forward and get into a rhythm. As the cutting proceeds you will find it necessary to raise the handle slightly to keep the cutting edge in contact with the wood. As the tool approaches the horizontal position the tool rest should be moved closer to the wood, to increase the tool angle again and reduce the gap between the wood and the tool rest.

Roughing with Spindle Roughing Gouge

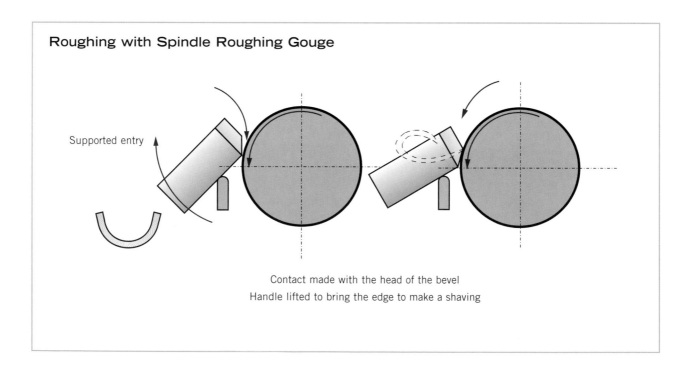

Supported entry

Contact made with the head of the bevel
Handle lifted to bring the edge to make a shaving

Roughing Cut

Tool square to the wood.
Slide backwards and forward
cutting continuously

10 When one part of the edge becomes blunt, twist
the tool to bring a sharp part of the cutting edge
into contact with the wood. If you have judged
it right, the square section should be completely
round. As this cut is across the grain, the finish
will not be very good, but it is a quick and
efficient way of removing wood.

Finishing cut

1 Lower the tool rest to ⅝in (16mm) below centre
height.

2 Swing the tool round to 45° to the axis, towards the
headstock, so that the bevel is parallel to the axis.
With flute facing forward, point the tool upwards
at about 20–30°. This is the position for a 'sheer
peeling' cut.

3 Stand in the same position as for the roughing cut.
At this point if you haven't already put your arm on
top of the headstock then now is the time to do it.

4 Move the tool away from the wood and switch on
the lathe. Bring the heel of the bevel into contact
with the wood and the cutting edge just away from
the wood.

5 Make the supported entry by slowly sliding the tool
forward along the rest. At the same time swing
the handle forward until the tip of the tool raises
a shaving, then continue to slide the tool slowly
along the rest, taking a fine shaving off all the way.

Tip
Draw a thick pencil line around the middle
of the square wood. The line will gradually
disappear as you turn, and when it is gone the
wood will be completely round.

6 Stop at the end of the cut and, keeping the
bevel in contact with the wood, slide the tool
back along to the other end to make another cut.
Keep repeating until the wood is as small as you
can make it. The finish will be very smooth and
straight. Throughout this process, your hand should
not have touched the tool rest, keeping control on
the bevel.

Finishing cut

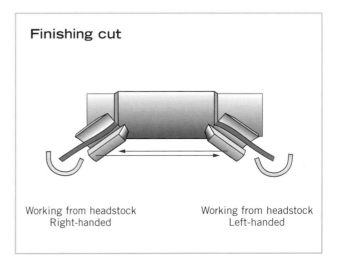

Working from headstock
Right-handed

Working from headstock
Left-handed

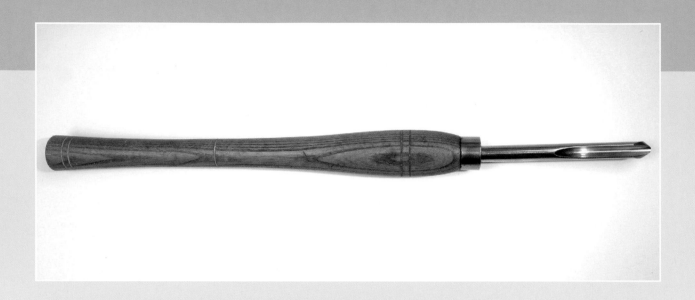

Deep-fluted gouge

The deep-fluted gouge (DFG) can remove a lot of wood and leave a very good finish at the same time. It is one of the turner's most versatile and easy-to-use tools. Its great strength is in cross-grain bowl turning but it also performs like magic on parallel grain spindle turning. The DFG can be used to turn many different shapes. They start with a direct or supported entry.

Making direct entry cuts

Set the lathe speed to 2,000rpm. Mount a piece of softwood, 2½in (63mm) square – equivalent to 3½in (89mm) diam – and 10in (254mm) long, between centres. Set the tool rest to ¾in (19mm) below centre height, ½in (12mm) away from the wood and projecting 2in (50mm) beyond the end of the wood at the tailstock end.

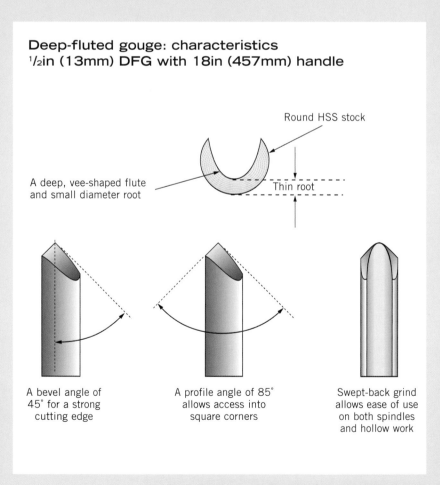

Deep-fluted gouge: characteristics
½in (13mm) DFG with 18in (457mm) handle

Round HSS stock

A deep, vee-shaped flute and small diameter root

Thin root

A bevel angle of 45° for a strong cutting edge

A profile angle of 85° allows access into square corners

Swept-back grind allows ease of use on both spindles and hollow work

Top A ½in (12mm) DFG has a stock diameter of ⅝in (15mm). An 18in (457mm) long handle gives ease of control and reduces the pressure required.

Using the DFG to square the ends of square stock produces sharp corners with no breakaway. Perfect results every time.

The glass-like, smooth finish and sharp corners on the chamfer are perfect – even on softwood.

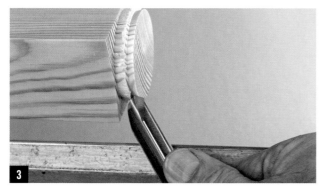

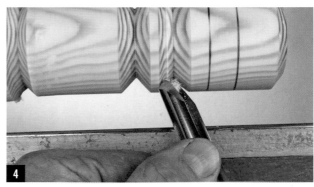

A profile angle of 85° makes cutting square or dovetail spigots quick and easy.

If the vee you want is 90° or greater, then you can use the DFG to make it in just three cuts.

Hollowing out end grain, working with the grain from the bottom outwards.

Turning a cross-grain bowl, working from base to rim. Cutting with the grain, the DFG flows over the wood leaving a smooth finish.

Turning the inside of a cross-grain bowl from the rim to the centre, working with the grain to create the perfect curve.

Turning thin stems. Even on delicate spindle work, the DFG allows fine control along the long thin stems.

Power grip for the control hand. Thumbs-up grip and fingers of the support hand against the rest.

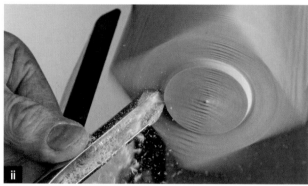

Slowly feed the edge into the wood by pushing with the thumb of the support hand.

Squaring ends

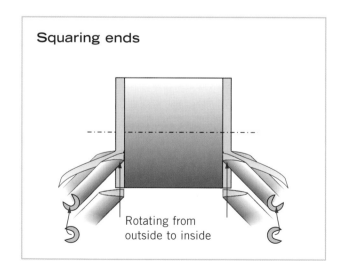

Rotating from outside to inside

1 Draw on a series of lines, ¼in (6mm) apart.

2 Put the DFG on the tool rest, line up the bevel with the direction of cut at the first line. With the flute at 90°, point the gouge to the axis of the lathe.

3 Stand behind the tool, in a dynamic stance, in the direction of cut. Hold the tool using power grip for the control hand; for the support hand use thumbs-up grip and place fingers against the rest. **(i)**

4 Switch on the lathe.

5 Slowly feed the edge into the wood by pushing with the thumb of the support hand and the control hand, in line with the bevel. **(ii)**

6 Once bevel contact has been made – about ¼in (6mm) on square section – twist the tool 45° to the cutting attitude (half open).

7 Continue the cut until you reach ½in (12mm) diameter.

8 Slide the tool back along the cut surface to the beginning and repeat the cut on the next line.

9 Repeat steps 5–8 at the other end of the wood. You will notice that the hands on the tool change but don't fight this – it is absolutely essential to be able to use both hands.

Making a chamfer

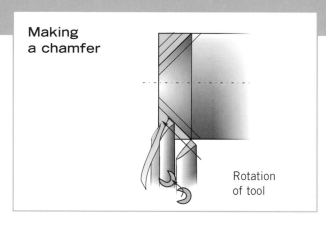

Rotation of tool

Making a second cut, in exactly the same way as the first, to the centre of the vee.

Putting on a 45° chamfer

1 Follow the procedure as for squaring the spindle end, only this time line up the bevel at 45° to the lathe axis.

2 Make a series of cuts flowing from one to the next. The finish will be smooth and clean with sharp edges at the start and finish.

Turning a 90° vee in three cuts

Vees are blind cuts, where the cut stops in a corner. You need to aim for a sharp corner to finish. The gouge will only make a sharp corner with the flute in the 90° attitude (closed). So the sequence of tool attitude is: 90° for the direct entry; 45° for the cut; 90° to finish.

1 Draw three lines on the wood ½in (12mm) apart to position the vee. Line up the bevel at 45° to the axis, at one of the outside lines pointing towards

the centre of the vee. Start cut 1 exactly as for the chamfer and when the cut is almost full depth, twist the tool to the 90° attitude (closed).

2 Without moving, hold the tool in exactly the same way and twist 180° to start the second cut on the opposite side of the vee. This time do not change hands – these are short detail cuts and changing hands would be unnecessarily clumsy. Make cut 2 in exactly the same way as the first, to the centre of the vee. Leave just a little to clean up on the opposite face and take care not to cut into the finished face. (i)

3 For cut 3 twist the tool back 180° and clean out the little bit in the bottom to make a clean vee. This quick and simple three-cut sequence is one worth practising. Never do a fourth cut – just practise getting it right first time.

Turning a vee in three cuts

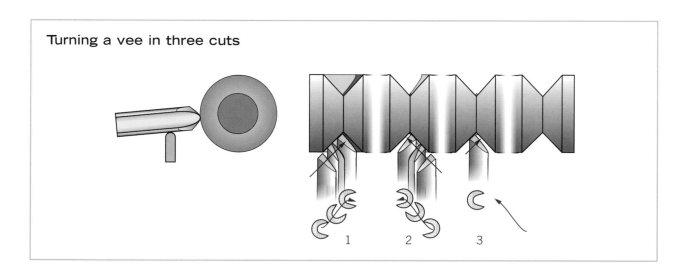

1   2   3

Cross-grain bowls

1 Direct entry is made, exactly the same as before. Once into the wood, change the grip of the control hand to either a back grip or a fingers grip, not touching the tool rest.

2 The shape of the cut is then determined by the control hand swinging the handle backwards or forward as the cut proceeds. Initial turning on the single-screw chuck is left-handed **(i)**, then turning the inside is right-handed. **(ii)**

Turning cross-grain bowls

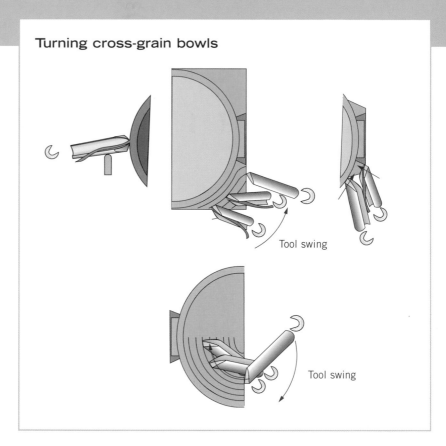

Tool swing

Tool swing

i

ii

Left Turning the outside of a cross-grain bowl. The left hand is the control hand.

End-grain bowls

1 In order to cut with the grain on the inside, the cut needs to be made from the centre outwards. Make a basic direct entry. Grip the tool tightly between the fingers and thumb of the support hand (thumbs-up grip), which should be held firmly against the tool rest.

2 Pivot the tool in the fingers to bring the cut around the base and up the side **(iii)**. This is a crude cut, which is poor on finish and shape control but very effective in wood removal. Depending on the wood being turned, the finishing cuts can be made against the grain (as if it is cross-grain) for a good shape and finish.

Left Turning the inside of the bowl; this time the right hand is the control hand.

Turning end-grain bowls

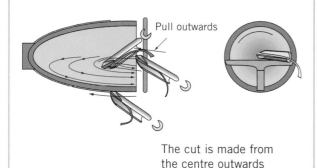

Pull outwards

The cut is made from the centre outwards

iii

Making a second cut, in exactly the same way as the first, to the centre of the vee.

Supported entry

Contact made with the heel of the tool. The tool is then slid and swung forward until a shaving is raised, then the cut continued

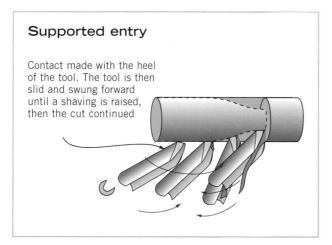

Tip
Whether direct or support entry is made, directional control is the same. Once the tool is in the wood, swing the handle to control direction, on both spindle and cross-grain work.

Supported entry
Supported entry is used when there is a smooth change of surface direction. These long cuts are good for practising tool control, although they are more likely to be used on bowls.

Making supported entry cuts
1 Place the tool on the rest about 1in (25mm) in from the near end of the wood. The tool should be roughly facing the direction of cut with the flute at 45° (open).

2 Stand behind the tool in a dynamic stance. Use power grip on the control hand. The fingers of the support hand should press the tool and hold the bevel against the wood.

3 Contact the heel of the bevel on the wood. Slide the tool forward, using both the control hand and the fingers of the support hand, while swinging the handle forward until the cutting edge makes a shaving. Keep the direction into the wood until the depth of cut is ⅛in (3mm), then swing the handle back to bring the bevel parallel to the axis and continue to the end of the wood.

4 Stop and slide the tool back along the surface to the beginning and repeat the process. Get into a rhythm of making the cut then sliding back to make the next cut – this is the important part of the process.

5 If there is enough wood left, repeat the cut but this time gradually remove the fingers of the support hand and push with the control hand so the cut continues with just the one hand. Replace the support hand fingers for the last 1in (25mm) of the cut and slowly go through to the end. Turning single-handed isn't a party trick, it is an important part of understanding what each hand contributes to the process. Practise pushing, pulling, pressing on the tool for stability – whatever it takes to refine the cut. Then, when you can take away the support hand for some cuts, you will have got it just right.

Shallow-fluted gouge

The shallow-fluted gouge (SFG) is a fine, delicate tool for detail work, primarily for spindle turning and making detail cuts such as beads, vees and coves.

Best for making short, straight cuts and curves rather than long cuts, it can also be used for finishing cuts on shallow bowls. The fine 30° bevel angle puts the handle more in line with the direction of cut than the 45° bevel on the DFG. Its 45° profile angle allows it to make narrow vees.

Basic cuts
The basic direct entry cuts made with the SFG are similar to those made with the DFG: line the bevel up in the direction of cut, then feed the edge into the wood. Set the lathe speed to 2,000rpm. Mount a piece of softwood, 2½in (63mm) square – equivalent to 3½in (89mm) dia – and 10in

Top ½in (12mm) shallow-fluted gouge with 15in (381mm) handle.

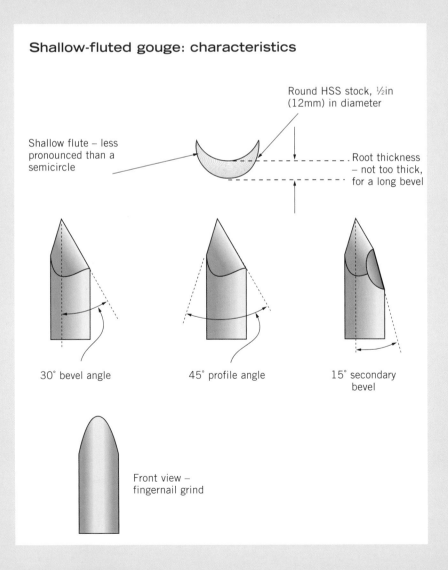

Shallow-fluted gouge: characteristics

Round HSS stock, ½in (12mm) in diameter

Shallow flute – less pronounced than a semicircle

Root thickness – not too thick, for a long bevel

30° bevel angle

45° profile angle

15° secondary bevel

Front view – fingernail grind

Cutting square ends.

Cutting chamfers.

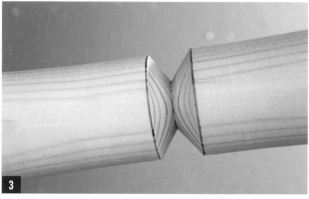

Making vees.

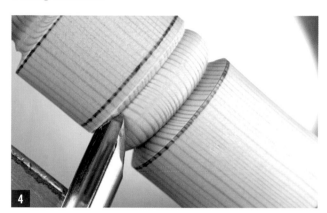

Cutting beads.

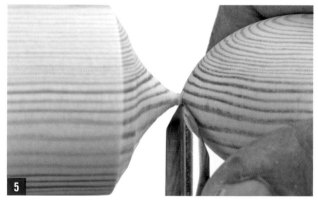

Parting.

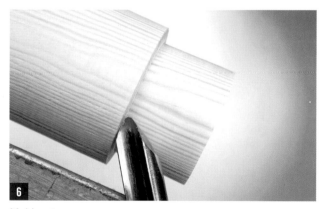

Making tenons.

Cutting coves.

Hollowing end grain.

131

(254mm) long, between centres (or a shorter piece can be held in a chuck). Set the tool rest to ⅜–½in (9–12mm) below centre height, ½in (12mm) away from the wood. Draw a series of lines on the wood for the particular cut.

Making a basic cut

1 Place the tool on the rest with the tip of the cutting edge vertical (flute closed). Line up the bevel with the direction of cut and point the centre of the flute towards the axis of the lathe.

2 Stand behind the tool in a dynamic stance. Hold the handle in the power grip and hold the stock in the thumbs-up grip. Point the tip to the lathe axis. **(i)**

3 Slowly but firmly push the cutting edge into the wood with the thumb of the support hand. Once the cut has been established, twist the gouge about 10° (open the flute). If the cut goes into a corner, then the tool should be returned to the closed attitude at the end of the cut, to obtain a sharp corner.

For the following cuts, the procedure is the same, but with these additions.

Square cuts

1 Draw on lines no more than ⅛in (3mm) apart.
2 Line up the bevel at 90° to the axis. **(ii)**

Power grip and thumbs up.

Squaring the end of a spindle.

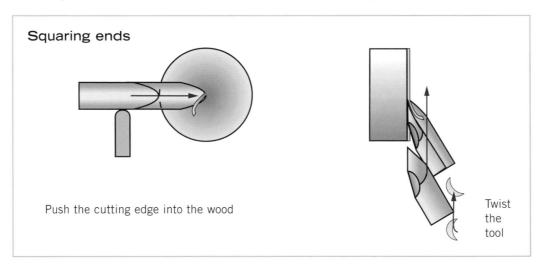

Squaring ends

Push the cutting edge into the wood

Twist the tool

Making a chamfer

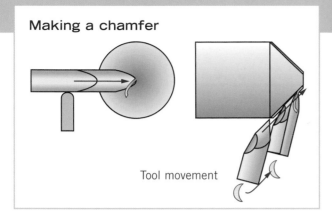

Tool movement

Making a chamfer.

Chamfers

1 Draw on lines no more than ⅛in (3mm) apart at one end of the wood.

2 Line up the bevel at the chamfer angle of 45°, in line with the first mark. **(i)**

Vees

1 Vee cuts are made up of a series of chamfer cuts on alternate sides. Draw three lines ¼in (6mm) apart to locate the vee. Add intermediate lines ⅛in (3mm) apart.

2 Line up the bevel with the first mark on one side of the vee, at 60° to the lathe axis. Make a fine cut almost to the centre line (the handle will be just about square to the axis). **(ii)**

3 Twist the tool 180° and line up the bevel with the first mark on the opposite side of the vee. Make a second fine cut to the centre line. Repeat the procedure with a series of fine cuts until the width has been reached. The last cut is a short one to clean up the corner.

Turning a vee.

Turning a vee

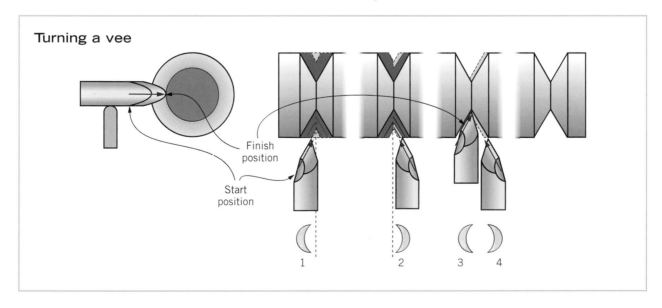

Finish position

Start position

1   2   3   4

Cutting beads and coves

Beads and coves require twisting and swinging the tool to complete the shape. There are two kinds of beads: inset and proud.

Inset beads

1 Set the tool rest to ½in (12mm) below the centre. Draw on five lines to represent the bead.

2 Hold the tool square to the axis, twisted slightly in the direction of cut, contact point about ⅛in (3mm) down from the tip, on the centre line.

3 Stand to one side – to the right if you are right-handed. Hold the tool handle in a flexi grip and the stock in a hook grip. **(i)**

4 With a positive action use both hands to twist the gouge while lifting the handle. The tip of the gouge should end up with the flute at 90° at the bottom of the cut.

5 Roll the tool back to the start position and repeat the cut on the opposite side. Make a vee cut on each side. Clean up with a short cut at the side of the bead. **(ii)**

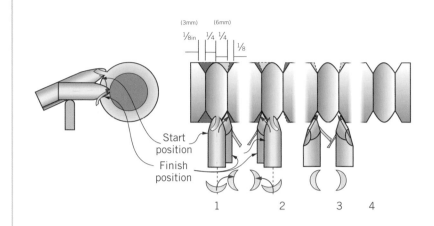

Turning an inset bead

Flexi and hook grips.

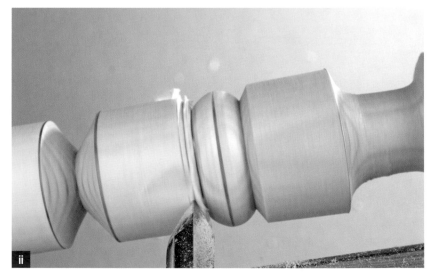

Turning an inset bead.

Cutting a proud bead

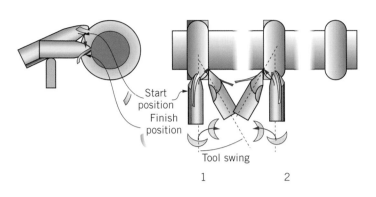

Start position
Finish position
Tool swing
1   2

Cutting a proud bead.

Proud beads

1 First clear space on both sides. Line up the gouge as for the inset bead, but this time swing the handle 30° so that the bevel ends up square to the axis, creating a hemispherical bead. **(i)**

Coves

1 Coves can be made in three cuts, starting with a direct entry, as for the straight cuts. Mark the location of the cove with three lines.

2 Place the tool in the finish position, square to the axis. Make bevel contact at the tip on the centre line.

3 Stand to one side – to the right if you are right-handed. Hold the handle using the flexi grip and hold the stock using the back grip, with the hand against the tool rest.

4 Swing the tool round to the start position, with the tool tip vertical (slicing cut). The bevel should be square to and pointing towards the axis.

5 With one movement push the tool into the wood, swinging and twisting the tool in an upwards scoop, until it makes the full depth of the cove and ends in the finish position. The gouge should be square to the axis, with bevel contact at the tip on the centre line. Next, repeat the process on the opposite side.

6 The third cut starts partway down the first side and is swung down to the finish position to blend in the cuts. Practise the three cuts so that you get it right first time. Any more than three will ruin the cove, unless it is a large one. **(ii)**

Cutting a cove

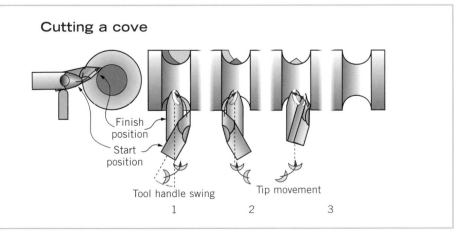

Finish position
Start position
Tool handle swing   Tip movement
1   2   3

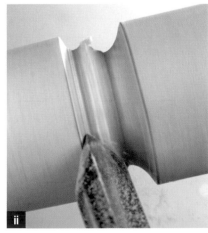

Turning a cove in three cuts.

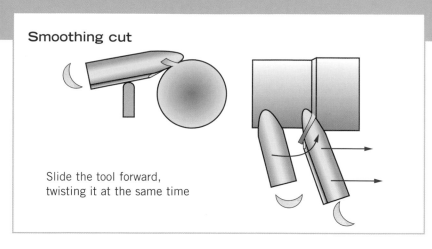

Smoothing cut

Slide the tool forward, twisting it at the same time

Making a smoothing cut.

Smoothing cut

For short lengths the SFG will put a perfect finish on a surface. Use 2in (50mm) diameter stock. Set the tool rest ⅜in (9mm) above the centre line, ½in (12mm) away from the wood.

1 Lay the bevel on the wood for supported entry. Use flexi grip on the handle, back grip on the stock. Swing the handle about 15° forward. **(i)**

2 Slide the tool forward, twisting it at the same time until a wood-shaving appears. Continue the slide to create a smooth surface.

Larger curve

Use this method for a curve that is too large to turn by twisting the tool, as when turning a bead. It can even be used for making fine cuts on bowls, with a direct entry.

1 Set the tool rest ⅜in (9mm) above the centre line, ½in (12mm) away from the wood. Lay the tool on the rest heel, contacting the wood, using power grip on the handle and back grip on the stock.

2 With the flute open about 10°, stand behind the tool in a dynamic stance. Slide the tool forward slowly, at the same time swinging the handle forward to start making a cut. Then continue the swing forward to create the curve. **(ii)**

Right Rounding a large curve.

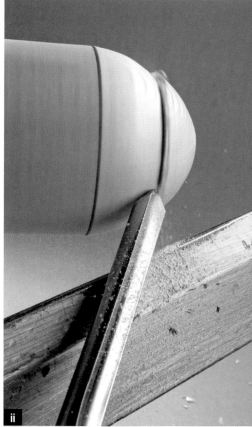

Rounding ends

Line shows tool swing

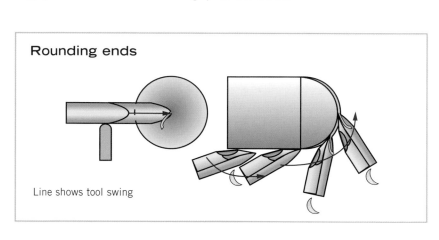

Skew chisel

The skew chisel is different from the other tools in that it has three distinct cutting parts which are used either separately or in sequence in the flow of a cut. They are: the long point, the long cutting edge and the short point at the heel. It is a very versatile tool which can complete many spindle projects on its own. This is the only chisel in the woodturner's armoury, its fine bevel angles give it access where other tools won't reach. (Well, I say it is the only chisel, but what is called a beading and parting tool is also a chisel.)

Top Skew chisel.

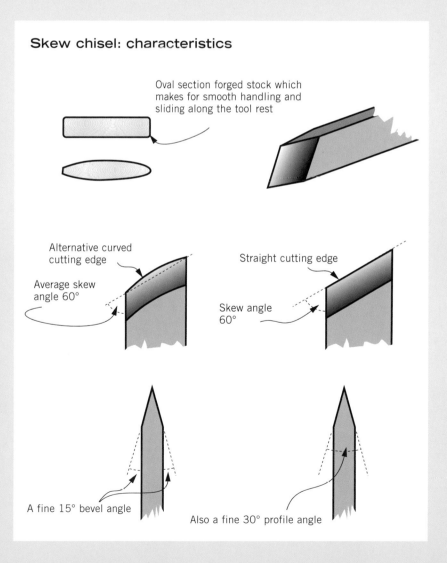

Skew chisel: characteristics

Oval section forged stock which makes for smooth handling and sliding along the tool rest

Alternative curved cutting edge

Average skew angle 60°

Straight cutting edge

Skew angle 60°

A fine 15° bevel angle

Also a fine 30° profile angle

Squaring the end of a spindle with the long point of the skew

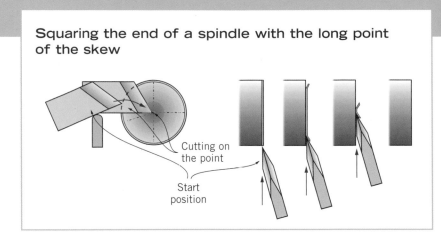

Cutting on the point

Start position

Squaring the end with the long point.

Long point – pointing cut

The point is used for squaring ends of spindles, chamfers and vees. In these cuts it is only the point of the tool that does the cutting.

Take a rounded piece of soft wood – 2in (51mm) diameter, 4–6in (102–152mm) long, 1in (25mm) wide rectangular skew chisel lathe speed 2,000rpm. Tool rest at centre line height, ½in (13mm) away from the wood, extending at least 2in (51mm) beyond the area to be cut. Put the long edge of the chisel (flat) on the rest with the tool upright. The skew of the chisel will ensure there is clearance between the long cutting edge and the finished surface.

Line up the bottom edge of the bevel in the direction of cut, to take a very thin cut. Stand behind the tool in a dynamic stance, facing the direction of cut. Hold the handle with the power grip. Back grip for the support hand, putting the back of the hand against the tool rest. An alternative grip is the hook grip. Raise the point about 20°–30° then firmly and slowly push the point into the wood, in line with the bevel, keeping the bottom edge of the bevel against the cut surface. Follow a straight line path with the point heading towards the centre line. Slide the tool out along the cut surface and repeat the process as necessary.

Squaring the end

As general procedure with:
Line up the bevel square to the lathe axis.

Chamfer 60°

Line up the bottom edge of the bevel with the angle of the chamfer to take a very fine cut (both the chamfer angle and the skew angle of the chisel will ensure there is clearance between the long cutting edge and the finished surface).

Chamfering with the long point of the chisel

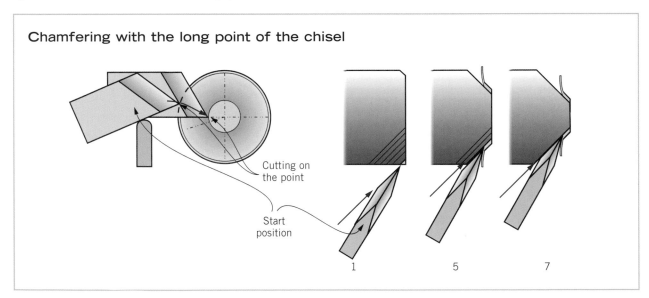

Cutting on the point

Start position

1   5   7

Using the long point to make a vee.

Vee

This a series of pointing cuts, as in a chamfer, on alternate sides of the vee. As general procedure with:

Power and hook grips while turning a vee.

1 Draw three lines on the wood ¼in (6mm) apart to represent the vee. Then intermediate lines not more than ¹⁄₁₆in (1mm) apart.

2 Line up the chisel square to the axis, raise the point (about 20°–30°), then, firmly and slowly, push the point into the wood. This does not produce a shaving, it just creates space for the further cuts.

3 For a narrow vee, swing just to the next mark on one side, make a cut then go to the next line on the other side and make a third cut.
Repeat these cuts on alternate sides (without changing your hands) until the width is achieved.

4 The last cut starts close in the bottom of the vee to clean up the corner.

5 For wider vees, swing the tool more to the left and right to make the cuts.

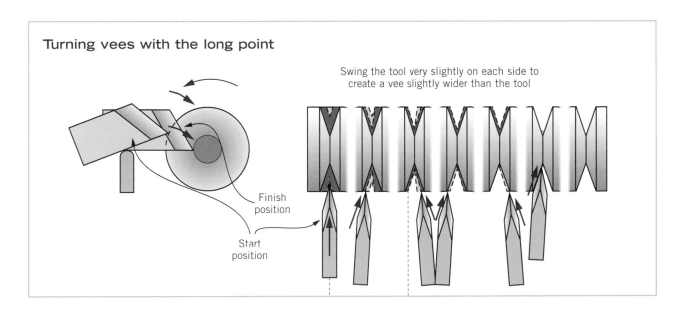

Turning vees with the long point

Swing the tool very slightly on each side to create a vee slightly wider than the tool

Finish position

Start position

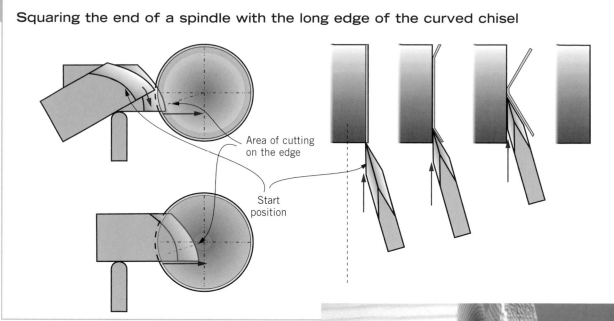

Squaring the end of a spindle with the long edge of the curved chisel

Area of cutting on the edge

Start position

Long cutting edge

General procedure for slicing cuts

Entry is made with one of the points, then the edge is brought into play. When the angle to the axis is less than 45° then entry is with the short point, when it is greater than 45° then entry is made with the long point. Take a rounded piece of soft wood, about 2in (51mm) in diameter, 4–6in (102–152mm) long and 1in (25mm) wide. Use a rectangular skew chisel. Lathe speed 2,000rpm.

1 The tool rest is ⅜–½in (10–13mm) below the centre line height, ½in (13mm) away from the wood, extending at least 2in (51mm) beyond the area to be cut.

2 Put the long edge of the chisel (flat) on the rest with the tool upright. The curve of the chisel will ensure that only a small section cuts the wood.

3 Line up the bevel in the direction of cut to take a very thin cut of ¹⁄₁₆in (1mm).

4 Stand behind the tool in a dynamic stance facing the direction of cut.

5 Hold the handle with the power grip. Back grip for the support hand, back of hand against the tool rest. An alternative grip is the hook grip.

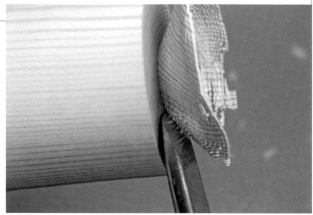

Squaring end-grain with the edge of a curved edge chisel

6 Raise the point (about 20°–30°), then firmly and slowly push the point into the wood. When about ⅛in (3mm) in, raise the handle to bring the tool horizontal so the cutting moves from the point to the centre of the cutting edge. Push the tool, following a straight line heading towards the centre line.

Squaring the end

1 Line up the bevel square to the lathe axis.

Warning

Only make this cut with the curved skew. This is one situation where only the curved edge skew can make the cut on the long edge.

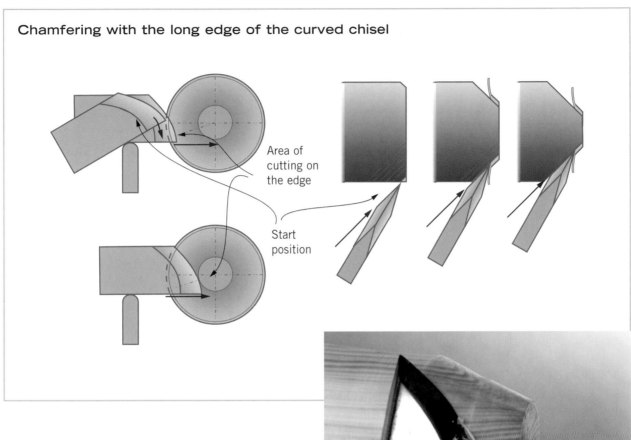

Chamfering with the long edge of the curved chisel

Area of cutting on the edge

Start position

Chamfer 60°
As general procedure with:
1 Line up bevel with angle of chamfer.

Smoothing and shaping cuts
This is a cut to make a long smooth finish on spindles, curves and beads – particularly soft woods.

Chamfering with the curved edge skew.

Warning
Make sure the chamfer angle is less than 70° before using a straight edged skew for this cut.

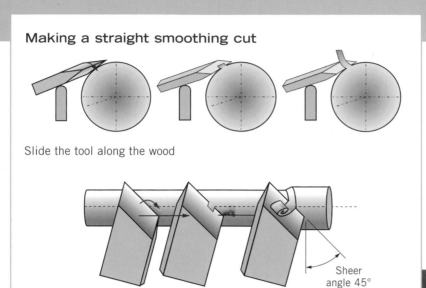

Making a straight smoothing cut

Slide the tool along the wood

Sheer
angle 45°

Smoothing cut along a spindle.

Smoothing cut

Set the tool rest at ¼–½in (6–13mm) above the centre line and ½in (13mm) away from the wood. Make contact with the heel of the bevel on the wood, set the edge to a 45° sheer peel angle. The centre of the cutting edge should be nearest to the wood, long point up. Stand behind the tool, looking down the line of the wood in a dynamic stance. The control hand holds the handle in a power grip. Support hand, with a fingers grip, pressing the chisel onto the wood and the rest.

Switch on, then, with both hands, slide the tool along the wood while slowly twisting the tool forward with the control hand until the cutting edge just takes a shaving. Keep the tool moving while taking the cut to the end of the piece. Slide the tool back to the start and repeat the cut as necessary.

Note
Keep the cutting at least ⅛in (3mm) away from both the top and bottom points. If the top point touches the wood, then the result is a dig in. If the bottom point touches the wood, the quality of the finish is slightly reduced. As the wood gets slim, the support hand can be moved to support the wood with the fingers while the thumb rests on top of the tool.

Power grip and fingers grip with arm over headstock.

Curves and beads

Curves
The skew chisel is twisted to change the bevel direction as the cut proceeds to create a curve. At the start of the cut, the tool is on its side with the bevel parallel to the lathe axis. At the end of the cut, the tool is on its edge with the bevel at 90° to the axis.

Procedure
A piece of 2in (51mm) diameter wood held in a chuck makes the other end free to cut a curve.

Draw lines from the edge, ¹⁄₁₆in (1mm) apart. Tool rest about ¼in (6mm) below centre line. Place the tool in the attitude for the end of the cut, long point up tool vertical and at 90° to the lathe axis. Hold the handle in a power grip, hold the stock in a hook grip, index finger hooked under the tool rest, stock held in firmly in fingertips or thumb. Then twist the tool back to the start position, ready to make the cut. Set the heel

touching the wood, at a sheer angle 30°–35°. Bring the cutting edge into contact with the wood on the first line. Chisel square to the lathe axis.

Move the tool forward while twisting and swinging with both hands and follow a curved shape. The support hand also holds the bevel against the wood. Keep twisting and swinging until the tool is in the end position. Repeat the cut from the next line until the curve is complete. The procedure for beads is almost the same as the curve above.

Hook grip while making a curve on the end of a spindle.

Turning a curved surface with either a curve or straight edged chisel

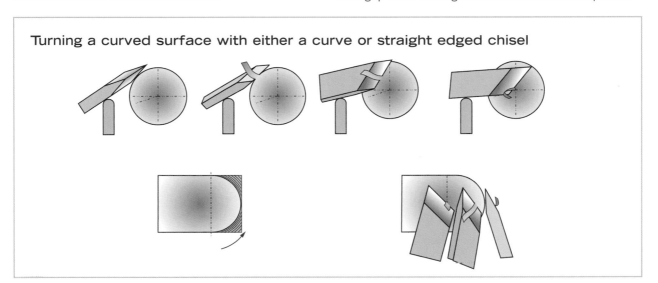

Rounding the corners on a proud bead.

Proud bead
The first side is exactly the same as the curve above. For the second side, keep the tool in the same hands and repeat the process in the opposite direction. For a small bead, only one cut on each side is needed.

Turning a proud bead with the long edge

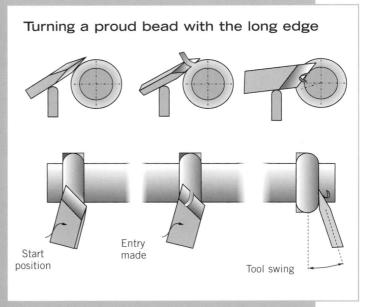

Start position

Entry made

Tool swing

143

Turning an inset bead in four cuts

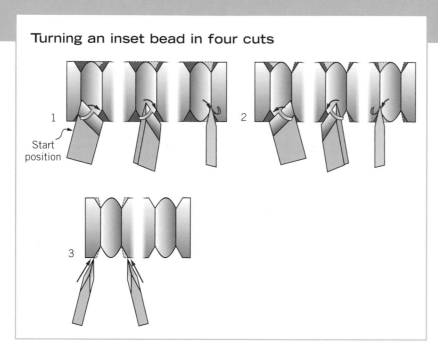

Make inset beads in just four cuts.

Inset bead

I like to make inset beads in just four cuts. It is a combination of making a vee and a curve.

1 Draw five lines on the wood ¼in (6mm) apart to represent the bead.

2 Make a curved cut on one side of the bead – twisting the tool but do not swing.

3 Repeat the cut on the opposite side of the bead.

4 Make a vee cut at each side with the long point. Larger beads will require more cuts.

Short point

When turning a round tenon with the long edge, as the cut approaches the corner then the tool is slid up the wood until the short point is cutting. The short point can be used to turn beads as an alternative to the long edge.

Curved edge skew

The curved skew is used in exactly the same situations as the straight skew, with the addition of two particular situations. Squaring the end of a spindle using the long cutting edge, the curve of the edge creates clearance at both ends, making it a safe cut. The second is making a smoothing cut into a corner, the edge can be swung round so that the curved edge completes the cut.

Turning to a corner with a curved or straight skew

Straight skew pushed up to bring cut on to the point

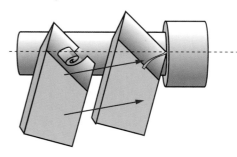

Curved skew swung round to cut into corner

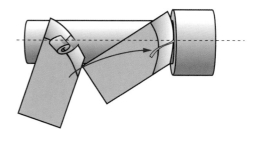

Scrapers

The major use of the scraper is as a finishing tool. It may only remove a little wood, but what little it does remove makes all the difference to the surface finish, and that's important.

Scrapers are specific tools, in that they cut shapes similar to that of the edge. Others are very specific, for example form tools such as thread cutting tools which only cut the shape of the edge. And it is because of this that I have more scrapers than gouges and chisels.

Scrapers are the one tool that sits flat on the tool rest, and the only rest they can do that with at all times is a straight tool rest. Curved tool rests make the scraper unstable and difficult to control. If the cutting edge is lowered there will only be a single point contact on the rest and the scraper will be rock. Also, if the tip is raised then the contact will be on the two corners of the tool stock and it won't slide easily over the rest.

Right Thread cutting tools, form tools.

Points of contact using a curved rest with a scraper

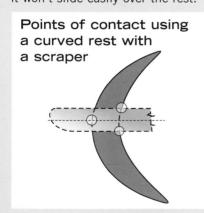

Scrapers: characteristics

Rectangular section with lower corners rounded for smooth handling and sliding along the tool rest

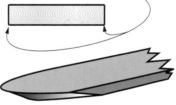

Left-hand curved shape suitable for bowls and goblets. With zero rake angle

A strong 45° bevel angle

Negative rake for potentially easier scraping

A strong 45° bevel angle

A selection of useful general shapes

Left skew square side cut scraper

Intersecting angle 85° (less than 90°)

Skew angle 70°

Right-hand skew scraper

Skew angle 40°

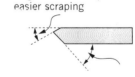

Half round scraper

Slightly domed scraper

Recommended handle lengths

Scraper width	Handle length
2in	24in
1½in	18in
1in	14in
¾in	12in
¼in	9in

Power grip on the handle and fingers on the stock.

Using – general principal

The heal of the support hand is on the tool rest while the tips of the fingers are on top of the scraper in a fingers grip. The first contact of the scraper on the wood should be with a floating entry, the cutting edge just touching the wood as the tool slides along the surface with a light but firm touch. The weight of the tool is a great help. Once contact is made, always keep the tool moving, sliding backwards and forward over the surface to refine the shape. At the end of the cut, gently pull the tool off the surface while it is moving.

But which one to use? From the tool descriptions you will see that I like large scrapers, ones that have some weight, stability and rigidity. Chose one where the shape of the cutting edge is closest to the shape being cut.

For a bowl or goblet use the left-hand curved scraper inside the bottom of a bowl, goblet or egg cup. The top of the tool rest just above the centre line height and the cutting edge should be on the centre line so that the centre can be turned. This gives a negative rake angle, so that any pull down on the tool by the wood results in the cutting edge swinging away from the wood with no risk of any dig in. The tool overhang should be large enough so that the tool angle is comfortable and that the full width of the tool is sitting on the rest to give support to the cutting edge. There is a lot of metal cut away below the cutting edge along the side of this tool and if this part of the stock sits on the tool rest, then there will be no support to the cutting edge and the tool would easily tip.

Where the wood is thin and likely to chatter, place the fingers on the outside surface of the vessel while the thumb sits on the tool to control it. The fingers

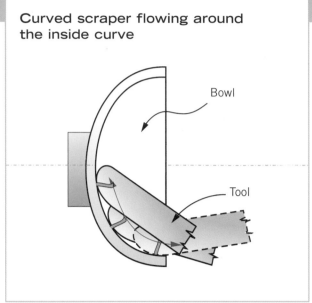

Curved scraper flowing around the inside curve

Bowl

Tool

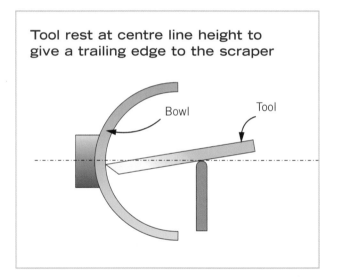

Tool rest at centre line height to give a trailing edge to the scraper

Bowl

Tool

Fingers behind supporting the wood, thumb on the tool.

follow the cutting edge, supporting the wood behind it. As the cut gets out of reach for the fingers, then revert to the unsupported method of holding.

On the outside of a convex curve such as a bowl, use a straight edged scraper with either a square or skewed cutting edge. Set the tool rest ¼in – ½in (6–13mm) below centre height, and about ½in (13mm) away from the wood at the nearest point. Assuming the bowl foot is in the headstock, hold the handle in the left hand in a flexi grip, the handle raised slightly to create a negative rake angle. Put the right hand against the rest and the tips of the fingers on top of the scraper to control the tool.

A more recent development in scraper sharpening is negative rake sharpening. This means grinding a negative angle of about 30° on the top of the scraper, then sharpening on the bevel. It is claimed that the negative rake scraper does not pull the wood onto the tool and so makes it a friendly tool to use – even on very thin work.

Left and right hand skewed straight scrapers refining the outside

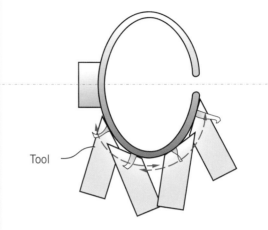

Tool

Sheer scraping is a particular scraping action, to give a very fine finish. On the outside of a cross-grained bowl use a right hand skewed straight edged scraper and twist the tool between 45° and 80° (sheer angle) so that it faces from the base to the rim.

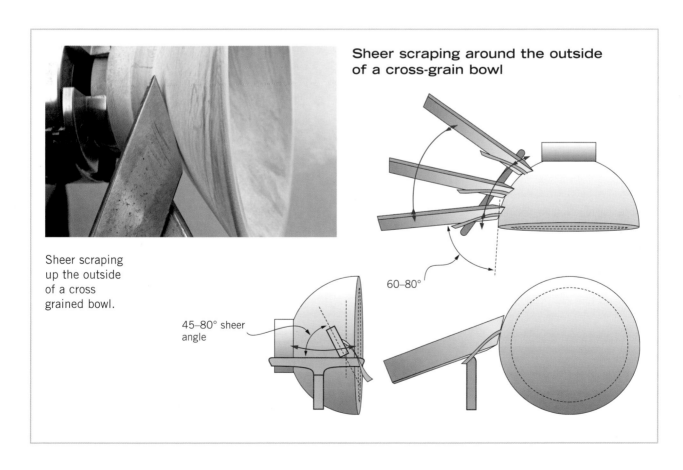

Sheer scraping up the outside of a cross grained bowl.

Sheer scraping around the outside of a cross-grain bowl

60–80°

45–80° sheer angle

147

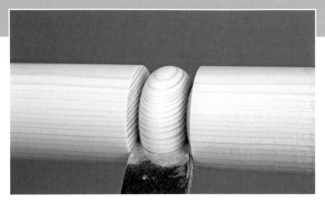

Cutting a bead with a bead form tool.

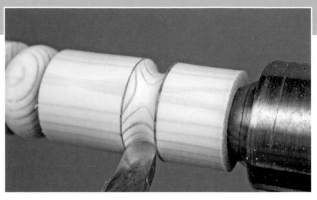

Cutting a cove with a cove form tool.

Raise or lower the handle so that the middle of the cutting edge makes contact with the wood. Swing the handle so the angle between the face of the stock and the wood is less than 90° (negative cutting angle) presentation of the cutting edge. Stand in a very dynamic stance, facing the top of the tool. With arms outstretched, hold the handle in a power grip, supporting the forearm on the tool rest with fingers around the tool stock. This is a whole body movement. Bring the cutting edge into contact with the wood with a floating entry, then swing backwards and forward to continue the cut. The cutting edge should float across the surface and should always be moving. The shavings that come off will be very fine and long, giving a satisfying feeling while cutting.

Form tools

Form tools are also scrapers, shaped and sharpened to create specific shapes such as beads, vees and coves. The tool is pushed in straight with a small waving so that not all of the cutting edge is in contact with the wood at one time. Take very light cuts and re-sharpen with a diamond file after each shape.

Cutting a vee with a vee-form tool.

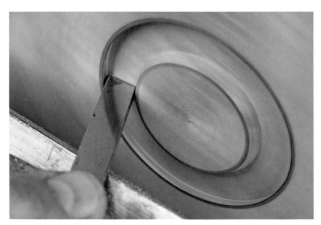

Turning a recess for an expanding chuck.

Turning a spigot for a chuck.

Parting, sizing and beading tools

Four very similar tools in section and sharpening, could almost be interchangeable, but slight variations give them their specific characteristics.

Parting tool

A separation process, either separating two pieces or separating a piece from the waste wood. We also want to leave a good finish on one or both surfaces and in some cases remove as little wood as possible where the wood is precious in terms that it is valuable or there is little wood left to complete the object. Also important when making boxes where the grain is to match.

Using the tool

Leave the lathe speed the same as used for turning and set up the tool rest parallel to the lathe axis and

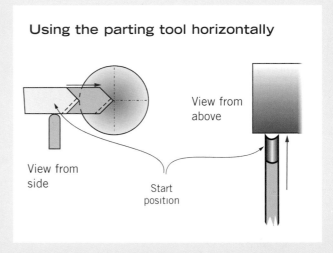

Using the parting tool horizontally

View from side

Start position

View from above

½in (13mm) away, below the axis so that the points of the parting tool are at centre height. With the tool at 90° to the axis, slowly but firmly push the points into the wood.

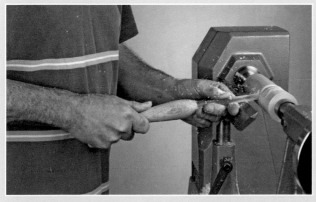

Holding the parting tool, power grip and back grip.

Parting.

Parting

Rectangular section

Round bottom corners for a smooth slide on the rest

Fluted on the corner of the grindstone

View 'A-A'

A

A

⅛in (3mm)

Bevel angles 45°

Sizing tool

Rectangular section

Round all corners for a smooth slide on the rest

⅛–³⁄₁₆in (3–4.5mm)

Bevel angles 45–30°

Bedan

Rectangular section

Round bottom corners for a smooth slide on the rest

⅜in (10mm)

Bevel angle 30°

Beading tool

Rectangular section

Round all corners for a smooth slide on the rest

⅜in (10mm)

Bevel angles 45–30°

With the wood held between centres, there is no problem at the start of parting off because there is sufficient wood in front of the tool to support the force from the tailstock. But as the diameter reduces, the small area of wood remaining starts to compress, reducing the width of the gap and trapping the tool in the groove. There are two ways of minimizing this problem: the first is to reduce the pressure by slackening the tailstock hand wheel as the cut proceeds. The other is to make a second cut, widening the gap to greater than that of the tool. A combination of these is often the best option.

Stop before the wood starts to bend and break as the grain is likely to rip into the finished piece, or the flexing might damage the piece. Finish the parting with a knife or hand saw either with the lathe stopped or on the bench. Where the wood is held in a chuck, and the pieces are small, the parting cut is made completely through the wood to separate the pieces while holding the piece in the hand. The waste will remain in the chuck.

Sizing tool

Using the sizing tool in conjunction with a pair of callipers. I would recommend rounding the ends of the callipers so that they run smooth over the wood and don't dig in. Present the sizing tool horizontal in the same way as the parting tool.

Tool rest ½in (13mm) away, below the axis. Hold the tool with a power grip in the control hand, and the callipers in the support hand. Start the cut by pushing the tool into the wood, then, well before the cut is down to size, gently rest the callipers in the grove so that its own weight will cause it to drop over the wood when it is down to size.

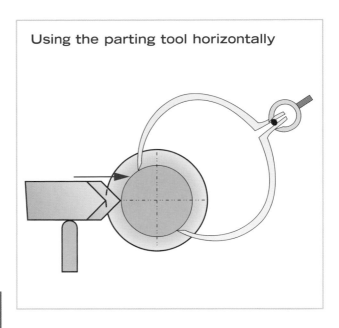

Using the parting tool horizontally

Left Holding the sizing tool and callipers.

Below Sizing with callipers.

Sizing with the bedan and sizing attachment.

Bedan

Tool rest below the axis. Set the sizing calliper to the diameter, place the tool on the rest, make the first contact on the wood with the hook of the calliper. Then slide it down the back of the wood, bringing the cutting edge to start cutting the wood. Keep the calliper pressed on the wood as the cut proceeds until the tool stops cutting and the size is reached.

Beading tool

This is basically a chisel and the points are used in a similar manner to the skew chisel. But its square section and large bevel angles make it a simpler and forgiving tool to use, though not so versatile.

Entry, supported entry: power grip with the control hand, back grip with the support hand. Make contact with the heel of the bevel at a slight angle, so that the point is leading, twist until the point makes contact and raises a shaving.

Bedan used with sizing attachment

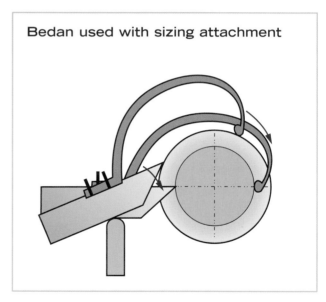

Entry

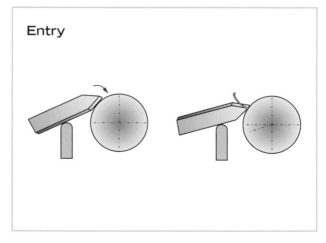

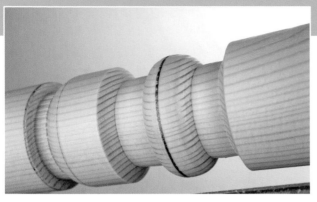

Bead made with the beading tool.

Rounding the end with the beading tool.

Beads

Make supported entry into the wood, then continue to twist and swing the tool to create the curve in a continuous flow.

Making short fillets

Make a supported entry, then continue to slide the tool into the corner to complete the fillet.

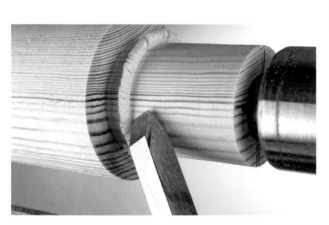

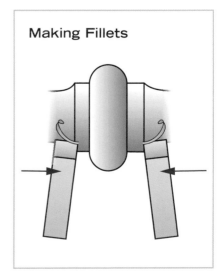

Rolling a bead with the point of the beading tool.

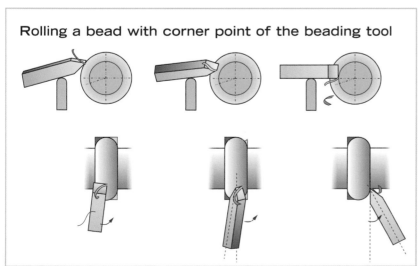

Rolling a bead with corner point of the beading tool

Making Fillets

Part four – Projects

When I am making one of a project, or a small run, I always cut two or three extra blanks, all exactly the same size. What this does is allow me not to worry about making mistakes, and that greatly reduces the chance of making a mistake. And if there is more than one stage in the turning process, I do turn the early stages on the extra blanks even though I might not need to finish them. This process greatly speeds up my turning and improves accuracy. With these six projects the planning is done, all you have to do is to make them. Select the tools from the tool rack, sharpen them, place them on a tray by the lathe, then arrange the abrasives and finish. Take the chuck or drive centres and fit them on the lathe. Mount the blank on the lathe and you are ready. Enjoy.

Bowl

Wood	Walnut, or select a close-grained hardwood with some interesting grain/colour Ash, elm, fruit wood or similar
Grain direction	Cross grain
Blank size	7½in diameter x 3in high (191 x 76mm)
Chucking method	Single screw; Spigot chuck. 80mm spigot jaws Wood jaws
Turning tools	DFG; ½in (13mm) Two Scrapers. Square straight – Left-hand curved 1½in (38mm)
Other tools	Pencil
Abrasives	100, (150), 180 and 240 grits
Finish	Lemon oil
Lathe speed	1,000–1,200rpm
Safety equipment	Face mask, goggles

Drilling for single screw.

Cut 1 Shaping the outside – DFG.

Procedure

1 Look at grain pattern and any faults in the wood to decide which is the top of the blank.

2 Drill hole for single screw chuck. **(i)**

3 Mount blank on the lathe, making sure it is securely fixed.

4 Draw a circle on the base to indicate the spigot diameter, which should be at least ¼in (6mm) larger than the finished base size.

5 **Cut 1.** Start cutting the shape from the small diameter to the large. Make a series of cuts creating the bowl shape. **(ii)**

6 **Cut 2.** Before you reach the line for the spigot, tale a light cut down the surface and re-mark the spigot size.

7 **Cut 3.** Make the spigot with the DFG.

8 **Cut 4**. Refine the shape down to the spigot – DFG.

9 **Cut 5.** Trim up the top face – DFG (not necessary if the face is flat).

10 **Cut 6** and **7**. Undercut the centre of the spigot leaving ½in (13mm) flat round the edge

Dimensions

7½in (191mm)

3in (76mm)

¼in (6mm)

Steps 5–6

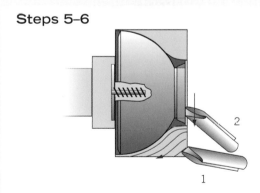

1

2

Steps 7–9

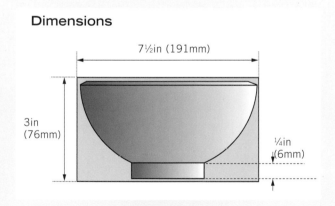

3

4

5

Step 10

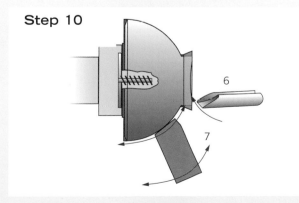

6

7

Cut 7 Refine shape with scraper.

Cut 10 Hollow inside.

Cut 10 Last cuts inside with fingers supporting the wood

Cut 11 Refine the inside with scraper, fingers supporting the wood.

11 **Cut 7.** Refine the outside shape with the large straight scraper. **(i)**

12 Turn the bowl round and hold in the spigot chuck. Make sure it is running true.

13 **Cut 8.** Trim the face with a light cut.

14 **Cut 9.** Make the chamfered rim by rolling the DFG in the peeling position (bevel contact under the cutting edge).

15 **Cut 10.** Hollow out the inside with the DFG. Last cut inside – fingers supporting the wood. **(ii+iii)**

16 **Cut 11.** Refine the shape with a large left hand curved scraper. Ensure your fingers are supporting bowl. **(iv)**

Steps 13–15

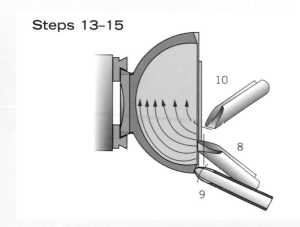

Step 14

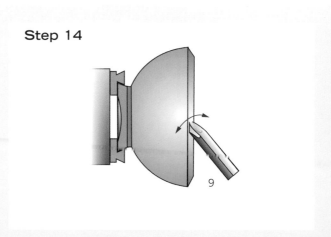

Sanding outside.

Reverse mounting on wood jaws.

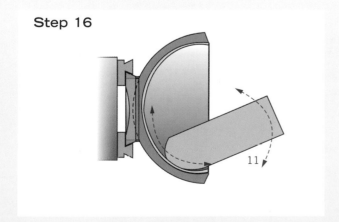
Cut 13 Shaping the foot.

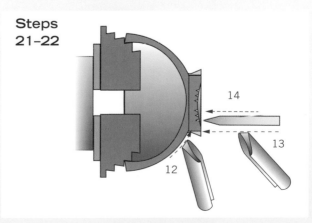
Friction drying polishing.

17 Switch on the dust extractor, put on some breathing protection and sand the outside 120, 180 and 240. **(v)**

18 Apply finish with a brush.

19 Friction dry/polish. **(vi)**

20 Hold bowl inside the rim on the wood jaw. **(vii)**

21 **Cut 12** and **13.** Turn the base and blend in the curve. **(viii)**

22 **Cut 14.** Add a little decoration with the point of a scraper.

23 Sand, apply the finish and remove from the lathe.

Step 16

Steps 21–22

Project 2

Lamp

Finished size	5in (127mm) dia x 11in (279mm) tall
Wood	Ash
Blank size	6in (152mm) dia x 1½in (38mm) 1½in (38mm) dia x 10½in (267mm) long (12in [305mm] if you are boring from one end only)
Chucking	Four prong centre
Revolving cone centre with removable point	⁵⁄₁₆in (7.5mm) dia
Counter bore	⁵⁄₁₆in (7.5mm)
Single screw chuck	
Expanding chuck	3in (76mm) diameter
Turning tools	
SRG	1¼in (31mm)
SFG	½in (13mm)
Deep-fluted gouge	½in (13mm)
Scraper, LH curve	1½in (38mm)
Scraper square	1½in (38mm)
Sizing tool	⅛in (3mm)
Parting tool	⅛in (3mm). Only if you are boring from one end
Boring auger	⁵⁄₁₆in (7.5mm)
Other tools	Callipers Pencil
Abrasives	120, 180 and 240 grits
Finish	Lacquer and wax
Lathe speed	1,200–1,500rpm for base and 1,800–2,000rpm for stem
Safety equipment	Face mask, goggles

Cut 1 Roughing with SRG.

Stem remounted on counter bore.

Procedure
Stem

1 Mark centres on the spindle.

2 Mount between centres – using a cup centre with a removable centre at the tailstock end.

3 Mount the piece, speed 1,800rpm.

4 **Cut 1.** Rough down to round with the SFG. **(i)**

5 Bore either from one, or both ends. **(ii)**

6 **Cut 2.** Remount with bottom end to headstock. **(iii)**

Cut 2 Boring through tailstock right along the stem.

Dimensions

10½in (267mm)
10in (254mm)
9¼in (235mm)
7in (178mm)
1½in (38mm)
⅞in (22mm)
(44mm)
1¾in
1¼in (32mm)
⅞in (22mm)

Lamp 1¼in (32mm)
Candlestick 1½in (38mm)

6½in (165mm)
1½in (38mm)
1¼in (32mm)
n (38mm)
⅝in (16mm)
⅛in (3mm)   ½in (13mm)

Step 4

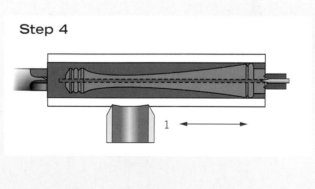

1

Steps 5–6

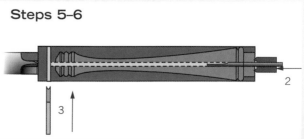

2

3

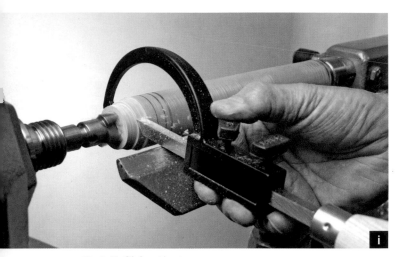

Cut 7 Sizing the tenon.

Cut 9 Turning the detail at the top with the spindle roughing gouge.

7 Mark out the positions of beads etc.

8 **Cuts 4–7.** Size the pin at the headstock end – 1¼in (30mm) diameter and other locations. **(i)**

9 **Cuts 8–10.** Turn the beads, with the SFG, then start the shapes between them. **(ii)**

Step 8

Step 9

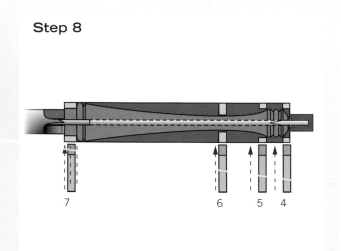

Cut 11 Shaping centre section between end detail with the spindle roughing gouge.

Cut 12 Turning the detail at the top with SFG.

10 **Cut 11.** Turn the body curve with the SFG. **(iii)**

11 Sand and apply the finish and polish.

12 **Cut 12.** Finish the top as close as possible to the tail centre. **(iv)**

13 Sand carefully 150, 180, 240.

Steps 10–12

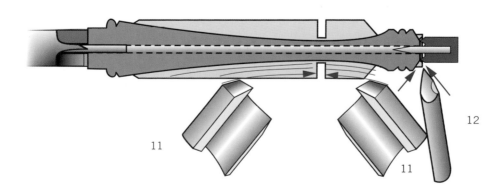

Cut 3 Making recess for expanding chuck.

Cut 4 Shaping top of base with DFG from centre to rim.

Cut 5 Refining top shape with large curved scraper.

Base

1 Mount the base on the single screw chuck.

2 **Cut 1.** Trim the diameter to round with the DFG.

3 **Cut 2.** Clean the face (slightly hollow) with DFG.

4 **Cut 3.** Make a recess for the expanding chuck with square skewed scraper. **(i)**

5 Sand and polish under the base.

6 Reverse the blank and mount on the expanding chuck. Mark in the diameters of the hole and flat area.

7 **Cut 4.** Shape the top face – cut from small diameter to large. **(ii)**

8 **Cut 5.** Refine with a large scraper. **(iii)**

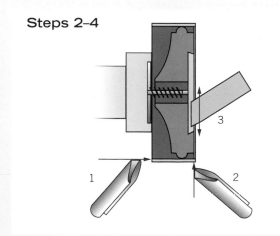

Steps 2–4

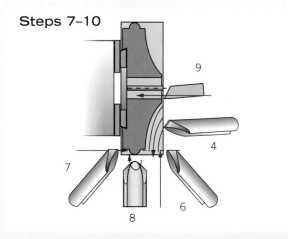

Steps 7–10

Cut 7 Clearing around the bead with DFG.

Cut 9 Boring for the lamp stem with square scraper.

9 **Cuts 6–8.** Clear the wood from the side of the bead and roll the bead with the DFG. **(iv)**

10 **Cut 9.** Hollow the centre to take the spigot on the spindle. **(v)**

11 Sand carefully 150, 180 240. **(vi)**

12 Apply the finishing oil and wax polish. **(vii and viii)**

13 Glue in the stem and hold in position with the tailstock.

Sanding detail.

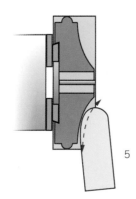

Step 8

Applying finish with brush – lathe running very slow.

Applying a carnauba hard wax.

Goblet

Project	Goblet
Finished size	2½in dia x 6in tall (64 x 152mm)
Wood	Apple
Wood selection	Straight grain wood will give strength to the stem and reduce the risk of it breaking during the turning process. If you are going to use wooden goblets then they should be made out of softwood as hardwood is porous.
Blank size	2¾ x 7in (70 x 178mm)
Chucking	Between centres – four prong centre + revolving cone centre Spigot chuck dia. 2in (51mm)
Lathe speed	1,200rpm
Turning tools	SRG 1¼in (32mm) Deep-fluted gouge ½in (13mm) Scraper LH curve 1½in (38mm) Parting tool ⅛in (3mm)
Other tools	Callipers, pencil
Abrasives	100, 150, 180, 240 and 400 grits
Finish	Liquid paraffin or finishing oil
Safety equipment	Face mask, goggles

Procedure

1 Put the blank between centres. **(i)**

2 **Cut 1.** Rough down square to the axis with the SRG, running up and down the wood until the blank is round.

3 **Cut 2.** Square end of the wood with the DFG. Hint: make sure the tailstock end is flat or slightly convex so that it will sit correctly in the jaws.

4 **Cuts 3** and **4.** Make the spigot, mark the size of the spigot with a pencil to suit your chuck at the tailstock end. Use DFG. **(ii)**

5 Remove the blank, fit the chuck. Hint: make sure it is good and tight.

Blank between centres.

Cut 4 Making the spigot.

Dimensions

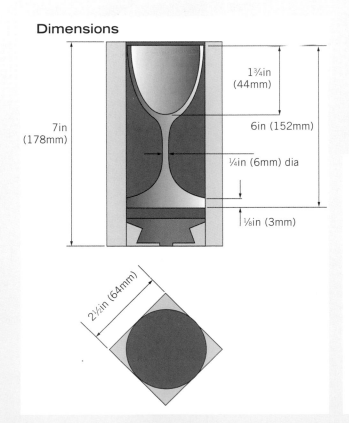

1¾in (44mm)

6in (152mm)

¼in (6mm) dia

7in (178mm)

⅛in (3mm)

2½in (64mm)

Steps 2–4

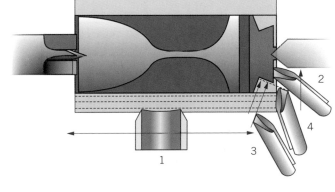

167

6 **Cuts 5** and **6.** Use the SRG in the finishing cut position to true up the blank if necessary. Make two cuts. One cut from the centre to the free end, then a second cut from the centre to the chuck end.

7 **Cut 7.** Square end, then mark the diameter to be hollowed out and the position of the foot.

8 **Cut 8.** With the DFG, hollow out with a series of cuts (either against the grain as per cut 8, or first rough with the grain as per cut 8a, then shape as per cut 8b). **(i and ii)**

Cut 8a. Hollowing with the grain from centre to rim.

Cut 8b. Hollowing from rim to base with DFG.

Steps 6–8

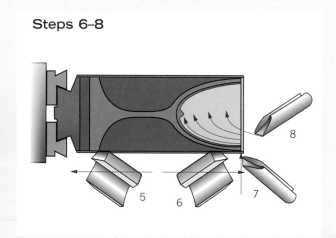

Steps 7–8

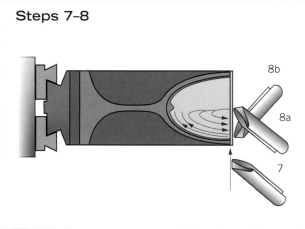

Cut 9. Refining the shape with large curved scraper.

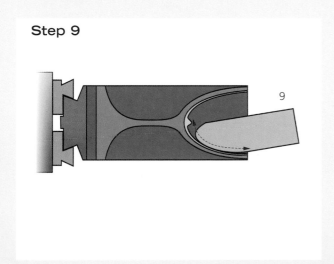

Cut 10 Shaping the outside of the bowl.

9 **Cut 9.** Take the scraper and refine the internal shape to finish the inside. Put a slight curved chamfer at the lip. **(iii)**

10 Sand the inside and top to a finish, softening the inside corner, and apply the finish.

11 **Cut 10.** Use the DFG to shape the outside of the bowl down to 1¼in (38mm) diameter. **(iv)**

Step 9

Step 11

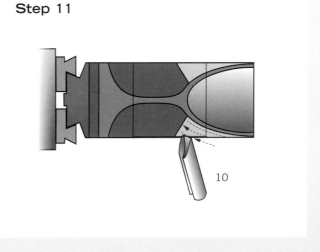

i

ii

Cut 14 Shaping the stem.

Sanding the stem.

12 **Cut 11.** Clear away some more wood. Hint: make this cut as if it is the finish cut for the top of the base – which it will be eventually.

13 **Cut 12.** Continue finishing cuts on the bowl, blending into the stem.

14 Start sanding the outside of the bowl with 100 grit. Use it full width and work up and down the cylinder. This will remove the high points and

make it smooth. Work through the finer grits until the surface is finished. Soften the lip corner with a fine abrasive. Apply finish.

15 **Cut 13.** Remove more wood along the stem with the DFG.

16 **Cut 14.** Make finishing cuts along the stem. **(i)**

17 Sand the stem as the finishing progresses. **(ii)**

Steps 12–13

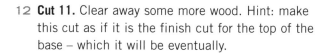

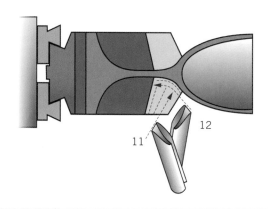

Steps 15–16

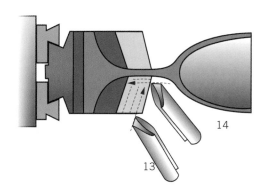

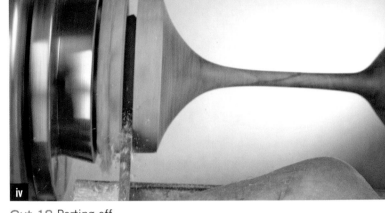

Cut 15 Shaping around the curve.

Cut 18 Parting off.

18 **Cut 15.** Make finishing cuts for the base and blend into the stem. **(iii)**

19 **Cut 16.** Clean up the side of the foot with the DFG.

20 **Cut 17.** Start parting; cut down 1in (25mm).

21 Sand and apply finish to the remainder of the goblet.

22 **Cut 18.** Part off – undercutting to make a stable base. **(iv)**

Steps 18–22

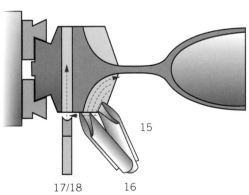

Project 4

Mushroom

Mushrooms in Irish yew.

Project	Mushroom (it is always best to turn the edible varieties)
Finished size	3–3½in (76–89mm) diameter x 4in (102mm) tall
Wood	Yew/Laburnum
Blank size	3–3½in (76–89mm) diameter x 5in (127mm) long branch Chose a clean irregular shaped branch
Chucking method	Between centres – four prong centre + revolving cone centre Spigot chuck diameter 2in (51mm)
Turning tools	
	SRG 1¼in (32mm) Shallow-fluted gouge ⅜in (10mm) Deep-fluted gouge ½in (13mm) Scraper 1in (25mm) Round/LH side cut
Other tools	Pencil
Abrasives	100, (150), 180 and 240 grits
Finish	Oil
Lathe speed	1,200–1,500rpm
Safety equipment	Face mask, goggles

Procedure

1 Hold between centres – top towards headstock. **(i)**

2 **Cuts 1** and **2.** Use the SRG to round both ends leaving 1in (25mm) wide strip of bark in the centre. **(ii)**

3 **Cuts 3** and **4.** Clean the end face and make a spigot 2in (50–60mm) diameter. **(iii)**

4 Fit into spigot chuck.

Branch between centres.

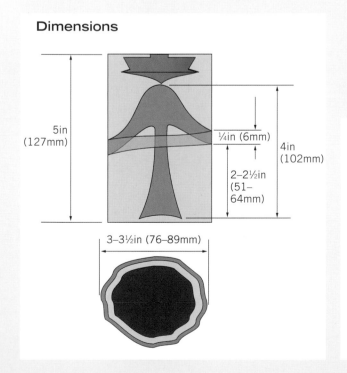

Cuts 1 and 2 Clearing bark at both ends with SFG.

Cut 4 Making the spigot – DFG.

Dimensions

5in (127mm)

¼in (6mm)

4in (102mm)

2–2½in (51–64mm)

3–3½in (76–89mm)

Steps 2–3

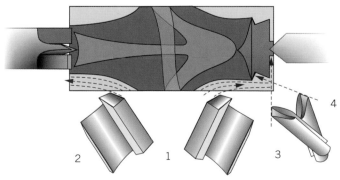

Cut 6 Roughing the stem – DFG.

Cut 7 Shaping the stem – DFG.

5 **Cut 5.** Undercut the foot – this not only looks nice but it is also more stable.

6 **Cuts 6** and **7.** Shape the stem up to the edge of the rim with the DFG. **(i and ii)**

7 **Cuts 8** and **9.** Undercut the rim and blend in with the stem. It is the angle of undercut that gives the rim its interesting shape. **(iii and iv)**

Cut 8 Undercutting the rim – DFG.

Cut 9 Continuing shaping the stem – DFG.

Steps 5–6

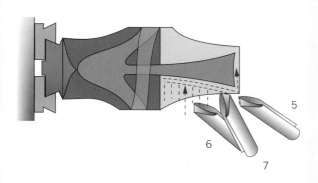

Step 7

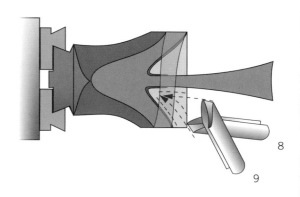

174

8 **Cut 10.** Refine undercut shape if necessary with a scraper. **(v)**

9 **Cut 11.** Shape the first section on the top of the mushroom. **(vi)**

10 Sand and apply the oil finish to the finished surfaces.

11 **Cuts 12** and **13.** Remove some waste (cut 12) and shape the top of the mushroom (cut 13), sand and apply finish before finally parting off with the SFG. **(vii)**

12 Hand sand the tip and oil.

Cut 10 Refining the undercut – with curved scraper.

Cut 11 Shaping the top – DFG.

Cut 13 Parting off – SFG.

Steps 8–9

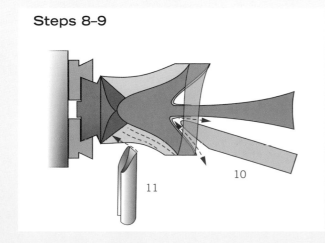

Step 11

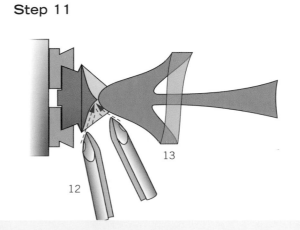

Project 5

Box

Finished box.

Project	Box
Finished size	2in high x 2in dia (50 x 50mm)
Blank size	2³⁄₁₆in sq x 3½in long (55 x 90mm)
Finish	Oil and wax
Chucking	Between centres – four prong centre + revolving cone centre Spigot chuck diameter 2in (51mm) Jam chuck
Turning tools	
	SRG 1¼in (32mm) Deep-fluted gouge ½in (13mm) Shallow-fluted gouge ½in (13mm) Scraper three various shapes – 1½in (38mm) Parting tool ⅛in (3mm)
Other tools	Callipers/measuring Pencil Dividers
Abrasives	150, 180, 240 and 400 grits
Lathe speed	1,200–1,500rpm
Safety equipment	Face mask, goggles

Procedure

1 **Cut 1.** Mount blank between centres. Round with SRG. **(i and ii)**

2 **Cuts 2–5.** Clean and put spigots on both ends. **(iii)**

Note

Turning the lid and base as laid out in the blank, and removing as little wood as possible from between them, means that the grains will match as closely as possible.

Blank between centres.

Cut 1 Smoothing with SRG.

Cut 5 Turning spigot on headstock end with DFG.

Dimensions

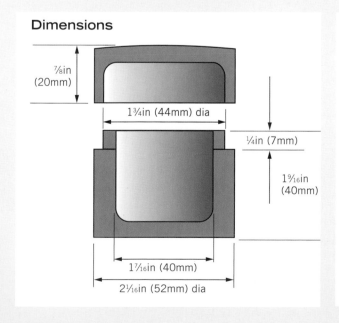

⅞in (20mm)

1¾in (44mm) dia

¼in (7mm)

1⁹⁄₁₆in (40mm)

1⁷⁄₁₆in (40mm)

2¹⁄₁₆in (52mm) dia

Steps 1–2

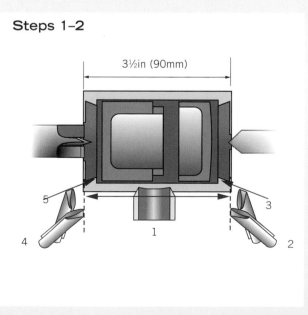

3½in (90mm)

5

4

1

3

2

Cut 6 Blank held in chuck – parting.

Cut 8 Hollowing lid from centre with SFG.

3 **Cut 6.** Mount top end in chuck and part off the base. **(i)**

4 **Cut 7.** Clean the surface, then mark on the joint face diameter. Use the point of the dividers to make a positive mark.

5 **Cut 8.** Hollow out roughly with the SFG working from the centre outwards. **(ii)**

Step 3

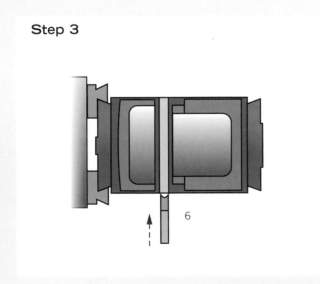

Steps 4–5

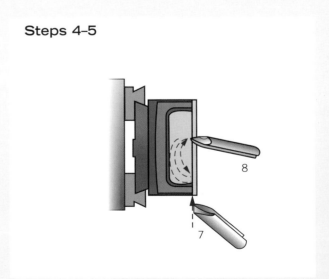

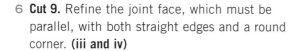

Cut 9 Refining inside lid shape and joint face shape with scraper.

Refining top face with scraper.

6 **Cut 9.** Refine the joint face, which must be parallel, with both straight edges and a round corner. **(iii and iv)**

7 Sand, oil and wax the inside and the end face to finish the inside completely. **(v)**

8 **Cut 10.** Part off.

9 Mount the base in the chuck. Measure the internal diameter of the lid. **(vi)**

10 **Cut 11.** Clean the face with the DFG.

Sanding – inside the lid.

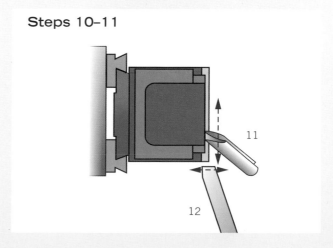

Measuring joint face diameter in lid.

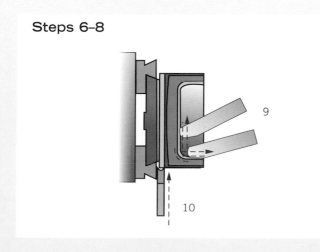

Steps 6–8

Steps 10–11

Cut 12 Turning short joint spigot on base with scraper.

Testing lid fit.

Making joint spigot full length.

Surfacing lid and base together with SFG.

Polishing with soft cloth.

11 **Cuts 12–13.** Make just a small lip of the joint to get the fit right – test with the lid – then complete the joint to full length. Again, test with lid. This procedure reduces the risk of losing the length of the joint if too much is taken off at the early stage. **(i–iii)**

12 **Cut 14.** Fit the lid on the base then make light cuts across the whole box with the SFG to make the side parallel. Face the tool to the headstock to minimize the risk of pushing off the lid. **(iv)**

13 **Cuts 15** and **16**. Take a light cut across the top of the lid to make it slightly doomed cut, refine with a large scraper and if necessary cut.

14 Sand, oil and wax the outside of the box then remove the lid which is completely finished. **(v)**

Step 11

13

Steps 12–13

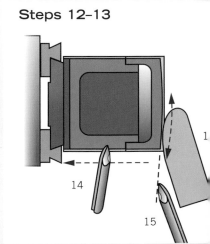

14

15

Cut 17 Hollowing the base with SFG.

Cut 18 Refining shape with scraper.

15 **Cuts 17** and **18.** Mark the diameter of the inside then proceed to hollow as for the lid cuts. **(vi and vii)**

16 **Cut 19.** Sand, oil and wax the inside, the top face, but not the joint face. **(viii)**

17 Fit another short piece of hard wood in the chuck and turn a short parallel spigot to fit the base. Covering the spigot with a thin piece of cloth could avoid damaging the internal finish. **(ix)**

Sanding inside.

Jam fitting base on spigot turned on waste.

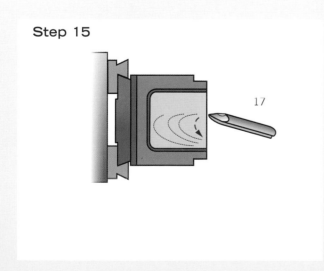

Step 15

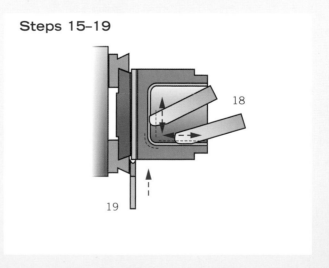

Steps 15–19

18 **Cuts 20** and **21.** Take a very light skim across the base, making sure it is absolutely flat or, better still, slightly hollow – cut 20. **(i)** Putting a little decoration on the base is a nice touch. **(ii)**

19 Sand, oil and wax the base (including the corner, which may be sharp).

20 Remove the base, fit the lid, line up the grain and that's a nice little box.

i

Cut 20 Clean under the base – DFG.

ii

Cut 21 Put detail marks under base with pointed scraper

Step 18

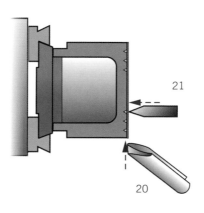

Project 6

Fruit

Project Fruit	Apple
Finished size	2⁹⁄₁₆in (65mm) dia x 2in (50mm) h
Wood	Irish Yew
Blank size	2¾in (70mm) sq x 3in (75mm) long
Chucking method	Between centres – four prong centre + revolving cone centre Spigot chuck with 2in (51mm) dia jaws Jam chuck – home-made
Turning tools SRG Deep-fluted gouge Scrapers Parting tool	 1¼in (32mm) ½in (13mm) 1½in (38mm) Left and right skew ⅛in (3mm)
Other tools	Pencil Jacobs chuck 3in (76mm) sanding pad and discs Drill bit – ⅛in (3mm) dia
Abrasives	100, (150), 180, 240 and 320 grits
Finish	Oil
Lathe speed	1,500rpm
Safety equipment	Face mask, goggles

Cut 1 Roughing square to round with SRG.

Cut 4 Turning the spigot.

Cut 5 Shape the bottom of the apple.

Procedure

1 Mark centres and mount in the lathe between centres.

2 **Cut 1.** Rough square to round with spindle roughing gouge. **(i)**

3 **Cuts 2–4.** Square the ends with the deep-fluted gouge (or SFG). Mark the diameter and turn the spigot. **(ii)**

4 **Cut 5.** Start shaping the bottom of the apple while still held between centres. **(iii)**

Dimensions

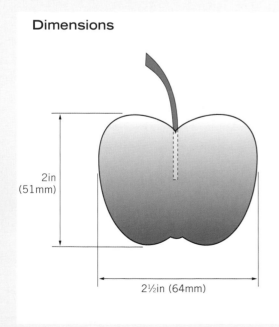

2in (51mm)

2½in (64mm)

Steps 2–4

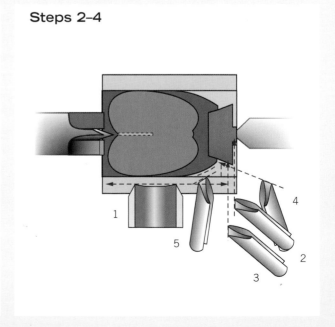

184

Cut 6 Following through shaping-top.

Cut 7 Shaping to base.

5 Remove the wood and centres. Fit the Vicmarc VM200 chuck and 2in (50mm) jaws. Fit the wood into the jaws and tighten.

6 **Cuts 6** and **7.** Shape the apple with the DFG. **(iv and v)**

7 **Cuts 8** and **9.** Refine the shape with skewed scrapers. **(vi)**

8 Now sand and apply the oil finish to the apple.

9 You can drill the stalk hole (size) from the tailstock at this point, or you can do it later by hand, which is what I do.

Cut 8 Final blending in.

Step 6

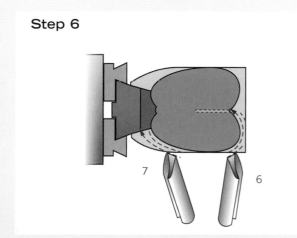

Step 7

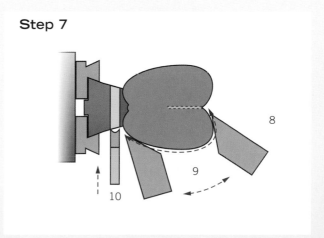

Cut 10 Parting with fluted parting tool.

Cut 11 Finishing under the base.

10 **Cut 10.** Part off with fluted parting tool. Allow to dry before fitting in to the jam chuck. **(i)**

11 Fit the jam chuck. Push in the apple top first with the palm of the hand. It does not matter if it is not quite straight as the apples will look more natural.

12 **Cut 11.** Shape around the bottom with the DFG. **(ii)**

13 A final sand around the base – blending to the finished surface. Apply an oil finish and friction dry.

14 A sharp tap with a tool on the side of the jam chuck should remove the apple.

15 If you haven't already, drill the hole for the stalk.

16 A nice touch on the bottom is to indent with triangular shapes in a circle to create a natural look.

17 The last part is the stalk, cut curved shapes on the band saw, **(iii)** then shape them on a small

sanding disc **(iv)** – start with 100, then finish with 240. Apply a finish to all but the end to be glued in the apple.

18 Use a thin glue such as Superglue to fix in the stalk.

However natural your apple may look, don't take a bite out of it!

Curved stalk blanks cut on the band saw.

Shaping the stalk on a sanding pad.

Step 16

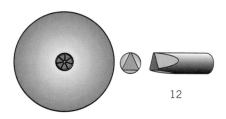

12

Metric Conversion Table

inches to millimetres and centimetres

in	mm	cm		in	cm		in	cm
1/8	3	0.3		9	22.9		30	76.2
1/4	6	0.6		10	25.4		31	78.7
3/8	10	1.0		11	27.9		32	81.3
1/2	13	1.3		12	30.5		33	83.8
5/8	16	1.6		13	33.0		34	86.4
3/4	19	1.9		14	35.6		35	88.9
7/8	22	2.2		15	38.1		36	91.4
1	25	2.5		16	40.6		37	94.0
1 1/4	32	3.2		17	43.2		38	96.5
1 1/2	38	3.8		18	45.7		39	99.1
1 3/4	44	4.4		19	48.3		40	101.6
2	51	5.1		20	50.8		41	104.1
2 1/2	64	6.4		21	53.3		42	106.7
3	76	7.6		22	55.9		43	109.2
3 1/2	89	8.9		23	58.4		44	111.8
4	102	10.2		24	61.0		45	114.3
4 1/2	114	11.4		25	63.5		46	116.8
5	127	12.7		26	66.0		47	119.4
6	152	15.2		27	68.6		48	121.9
7	178	17.8		28	71.1		49	124.5
8	203	20.3		29	73.7		50	127.0

About the author

After a career which began in engineering, including a spell as a research and development engineer in the nuclear industry, Michael and his wife Liz and children Cullen and Joanne took to the crofting life on Dunnet Head, the most northerly point on the Scottish mainland. Although Caithness is a windswept treeless landscape (well, almost) it became the basis for a new career in woodturning which has led to exhibiting and teaching around the world.

Acknowledgements

Thanks to the following businesses and individuals for their assistance: Vicmarc Machinery (www.vicmarc.com), Martin Weinbrecht, Drechselstube (www.drechselstube.de), Robert Sorby (www.robert–sorby.co.uk), Brimark Tools and Machinery (www.brimarc.com), Record Power (www.recordpower.co.uk), Saint-Gobain Abrasives (www.saint–gobain–superabrasives.co.uk), Liberon Ltd (www.liberon.co.uk), Crown Hand Tools Ltd (www.crownhandtools.ltd.uk), Craft Supplies UK (www.craft–supplies.co.uk), The ToolPost (www.toolpost.co.uk), Hegner UK Ltd (www.hegner.co.uk), Williamsons Chemists (Thurso, Caithness, Scotland), Charles Haughton (www.Tradcrafts.biz), Michael Barnett (Dunnet, Thurso, Caithness, Scotland),Ivor Thomas (John O'Groats, Caithness, Scotland), Chestnut Products (www.chestnutproducts.co.uk), Rustins Ltd (www.rustins.co.uk).

Photography by Michael O'Donnell, Joanne B Kaar and Liz O'Donnell. Other product images supplied by Record Power and Hegner UK. Drawings by Michael O'Donnell.

Index